Schumacher Briefing No. 2

CREATING SUSTAINABLE CITIES

Archit etc

D892

£ 4 —

Herbert Girardet

published by Green Books
for The Schumacher Society

First published in 1999
by Green Books Ltd
Foxhole, Dartington, Totnes,
Devon TQ9 6EB
www.greenbooks.co.uk
greenbooks@gn.apc.org

for The Schumacher Society
The CREATE Centre, Smeaton Road,
Bristol BS1 6XN
www.schumacher.org.uk
Tel/Fax: 0117 903 1081

Reprinted 2001, 2003, 2006, 2007

Cover design by Rick Lawrence

Digitally printed by ImprintDigital, UK

A catalogue record for this publication is available
from the British Library

ISBN 978 1 870098 77 9

CONTENTS

Foreword

I can't think of anyone more able to give us a vision of how we might try to start 'creating sustainable cities' than Herbert Girardet. Through his writing, his television programmes, his talks and his research, Herbert has been trying to identify the factors which can measure the success or failure of a city that is trying to become more sustainable.

The key theme of this book is the methodological approach of seeing cities as systems whose functioning needs to mimic natural systems. His work for London First enabled him to spend time collecting some key figures for London. Building on the work of William Rees and his colleagues, Herbert has calculated that London's ecological footprint requires around 125 times its surface area to sustain it. If this is extrapolated for all the mega-cities that are around the world today and in the future, then it is easy to see we have serious problems.

We are about to enter the urban century: for the first time, the majority of the world's population will live in urban areas. This will escalate over the next thirty years to the point when it is estimated by the UN Centre for Human Settlements that urban populations will grow to twice that of rural populations. Are we planning for this? No—we are not!

As a city dweller myself, I enjoy what urban life can bring. It does offer a cultural and social framework where I might express myself. In some northern countries, there are moves towards reducing traffic and reducing waste, to creating more pleasurable places to shop, eat and work.

Herbert shows that our present way of life in the developed countries is at the cost of others' ability to develop. Our model of development just doesn't work.

There are over 600 million people living in urban areas in developing countries-many live in poverty, suffer from pollution levels we would never accept, have insufficient waste management, inadequate provision of water, sanitation and drainage; their lives and health are under continuous threat.

Recently I was at the Department of Trade and Industry, where I heard a senior official speak of how Vietnam was developing. With pride in his voice, he explained that over two years ago, when coming from the airport in Ho Chi Minh City, the roads were full of bikes—and now you find yourself in a traffic jam!

If the growth in the use of cars is part of the development model we are promoting, then we have no chance. Curitiba, as we are reminded in this Briefing, has chosen a different path, where 75% of people go by bus to work.

I might add that when the problems with this growth in car use were pointed out, the official did understand. He just hadn't seen the connections-and that brings me to one of the points made in this Briefing about complexity. The more and more I think about it, the Earth Summit in 1992 was an enormously important event. Since Rio, we have been trying to get to grips with complexity and integration. Gary Lawrence, former Chief Planner in Seattle, said that "we should embrace complexity". This is easier said than done: since Rio, the forces of everyday politics try to push us away from complexity and integration towards 'seemingly simpler' sectoral approaches. If the debate on how we make our cities more sustainable is about anything, it is about how we embrace complexity at a local level.

As the booklet says, we do need a value base to work off and a set of objectives. It has to be about being, as Gus Speth, head of UNDP said, "pro-people (in particular, pro-poor and pro-women) and pro-environment. Being pro-people will, most importantly, mean development that is participatory and inclusive. Pro-jobs and pro-equality means allowing all people access to opportunities that development has to offer, including peace and security."

The booklet talks about a 'culture of sustainability'; Herbert calls, rightly, for a return to cities being centres of civilisation, not of mobilisation. For this we need vision and hope.

There are some good signs, as the Briefing says: the growth of over 4000 Local Agenda 21s is affecting how people see their towns and cities, and how they should be planned more sustainably. The sharing of good practice is going to mean that we all can learn from each other, though we do need a common methodological approach. The ability to measure our ecological footprint, or the collection of local sustainable development indicators, means that we can plan our policies better. We can start to learn to tread more carefully on this world. The urban century offers us considerable problems, but it also offers us hope, and the prospect of trying to find the solutions together. Perhaps the 21st century will be the century when humankind learns that we are all interrelated.

It was an Italian philosopher who said: "There is, nothing more difficult to take in hand, more perilous to conduct, or more uncertain in its success than to take a lead in the introduction of a new order of things." This Briefing, and the work of Herbert Girardet and others trying to map out how we should be creating sustainable cities, is part of 'a new order of things'.

Felix Dodds
Co-ordinator
UN Environment & Development Program UK

Preface

This short book is meant to make a positive contribution to the quest for sustainable development. The new millennium gives us a special opportunity to focus our minds on how the age of the city can also become an age of sustainability. I wish to contribute to this discussion in order to make some constructive suggestions, whilst I am also aware that the sustainable city is still a singularly elusive creature. The following text speaks for itself.

I wish to thank the people who have been involved in this project with me. James Robertson read a draft text and made some extremely helpful suggestions which I have tried to incorporate in the final text. John Elford, Director of Green Books, was similarly helpful in giving me new ideas which I have included in the manuscript. Felix Dodds wrote the Foreword at extremely short notice, and I am very grateful to him for this. I also wish to thank fellow members of the Schumacher Society Council, particularly Satish Kumar, Diana Schumacher, John Pontin, David Kingsley and Richard St. George, for discussing aspects of urban sustainable development with me and for encouraging me in this work. I wish to thank Natasha Nicholson and Pamela Charlick for designing the diagram on the metabolism of cities.

Published as the second Schumacher Briefing, I hope that this makes a useful contribution to the work of the Society and to the discussion on how to create a sustainable future. Since we have never been there before we may as well try our best to arrive there safely.

Herbert Girardet
1st January 1999

Introduction & Summary

At the end of the 20th century, humanity is involved in an unprecedented experiment: we are turning ourselves into an urban species. Large cities, not villages and towns, are becoming our main habitat. The cities of the 21st century are where human destiny will be played out, and where the future of the biosphere will be determined. There will be no sustainable world without sustainable cities. Can we make a world of cities viable in the long term—environmentally, socially as well as economically?

It is unlikely that the planet can accommodate an urbanised humanity which routinely draws resources from ever more distant hinterlands, or routinely uses the biosphere, the oceans and the atmosphere as a sink for its wastes. Can cities transform themselves into self-regulating, sustainable systems—not only in their internal functioning, but also in their relationships to the outside world? An answer to this question may be critical to the future well-being of the planet, as well as of humanity.

Human destiny is closely linked to the success or failure of the places where we live—cities, towns or villages. The history of human settlements is full of magnificent achievement as well as misery and despair. Many towns and cities have existed continuously for hundreds, even thousands of years, passing on the baton of urban stewardship from generation to generation. Others have dissolved into heaps of dust surrounded by desert. They imploded after devastating the local environments from which they drew their resources, or following social cataclysms and war. At a time when the majority of humanity is becoming urbanised, it is crucial to learn the lessons of history and to make sure that our settlements are socially just, participatory and economically viable whilst being environmentally sustainable.

For simplicity's sake I shall use the word *city* to encompass all human settlements, unless otherwise indicated. The definition of the word city varies greatly from country to country, depending on how much of the surrounding countryside is included. "For instance, the current population of most of the world's largest areas including London, Los Angeles, Shanghai, Beijing, Jakarta, Dhaka and Bombay can vary by many millions of inhabitants in any year, depending on which boundaries are used to define their populations." [1]

According to our own criteria, some 80 per cent of Europeans actually live in urban areas. Figures for North and South America and Australia are much the same. Africa and Asia still have a more even population distribution between city and country, though economic growth is rapidly changing the situation there too.

Global economic growth is closely associated with urbanisation. We are used to thinking of cities as places where most economic activity occurs and where great wealth is generated as a result. "The steady increase in the level or urbanisation since 1950 reflects the fact that the size of the world's economy has grown many times since then . . . " [2] It is clear that urban and economic growth are intimately linked. Not surprisingly, impacts on the natural world have increased vastly over the last decades. By my calculation, cities, built on only two per cent of the world's land surface, use some 75 per cent of the world's resources and discharge similar amounts of waste. This reflects the role of cities as engines of economic power whose commercial power depends on the exploitation and conversion of natural resources into consumer products.

In recent years the urban *social* agenda has dominated urban discussions: cities are uniquely human places and much effort has gone into addressing the problems of deprivation, alienation and crime and the welling up of social discontent. Cities as *cultural* centres have also received much attention. Great urban centres such as London, New York and Paris are widely celebrated as the epitome of cultural development. Environmental problems *within* cities in developing countries have been widely publicised, particularly those resulting from air pollution, inadequate sanitation and waste management, and poor working and housing conditions. Diseases such as cholera, typhoid and TB, well known in northern cities such as London 150 years ago, are now occurring in many developing cities, with epidemics threatening particularly the poorest communities.

However, an issue which has received much less thought is the huge *resource use* of modern cities and the resulting *urban wastes*. World-wide, urban development is closely associated with increased resource consumption. Compared with rural dwellers, city people in developing countries have much higher levels of consumption, with massively increased throughput of fossil fuels, metals, timber, meat and manufactured products. Yet cities *could* change. They *could* make efficient use of resources. How can we assure that appropriate policies and popular initiatives to achieve this potential will be implemented?

Historically, most cities grew and prospered by assuring supplies of food and forest products from the surrounding countryside, harnessing the fertility of their local hinterland. This is true of medieval European cities with their concentric rings of market gardens, forests, orchards, farm and grazing land, as well as of many cities in Asia, where this practice continues even in the face of rapid modernisation.[3] Future cities can learn a great deal from this model even if we cannot simply transplant traditional practices into the 21st century unchanged.

"If we would lay a new foundation for urban life, we must understand the historic nature of the city."— Lewis Mumford, *The City in History*, 1966.

Modern cities function very differently from the way cities did in the past. Low transport costs based on the ubiquitous use of fossil fuels have rendered distances irrelevant, plugging cities into an increasingly global hinterland. The process is often facilitated by substantial government subsidies on transport infrastructure.[4] The actual location of settlements is becoming less important as global trade treaties come to determine the fate of national and local economies. Many traditional villages no longer use the fertility of surrounding farmland and forests as their main economic base. All over the western world they are increasingly becoming dormitories for people who commute to work elsewhere or who use telecommunications as their main medium for income generation. Moving people and goods around long distance is becoming the norm.

Today we don't really live in a *civilisation*, but in a *mobilisation*— of natural resources, people and products. Cities are the nodes from which mobility emanates: along roads, railway networks, aircraft routes and telephone lines. Cities also sprawl ever outwards along urban motorways and railway lines to their suburbs and shopping malls and beyond whilst their centre is often devoid of life outside business hours. They are both the origin and the destination of this *mobilisation* which has come to define human existence.

Modern cities, as centres of mobilisation, have vast environmental impacts. Yet it is becoming apparent that, with appropriate measures, cities could prosper with a dramatic reduction in resource and energy consumption. Waste recycling can vastly reduce urban use of resources whilst creating many new jobs. New materials and architectural designs can greatly improve the environmental performance of urban buildings. Cities can adopt imaginative new approaches to transport planning and management, and to the use of urban space. We can dramatically improve the experience of urban living by the creation of new urban villages, reducing peoples' desire to escape from the pressures of city life.

Can we make *civilisation* come back to life again? Can we put the pulsing heart of conviviality back into our cities? How can we make sure of creating *cities of diversity* for the new millennium—places of cultural vigour, of lively encounters and physical beauty that are also sustainable in economic and environmental terms?

It is the task of this Schumacher Briefing to outline realistic options for change. The tools, techniques and partnerships that can help us achieve environmental and social sustainability and human well-being in the age of the city will also be central to creating a sustainable relationship between people and planet. In addition, we need to remind ourselves that cities aren't only places for humans, but that city people co-exist with trees, plants and animals that need their own distinct urban habitats.

Agenda 21, the main product of the Rio Earth Summit in 1992, emphasises that many of the world's environmental problems can and must be solved through active partnerships at the local level—in our settlements. Local Agenda 21 is the major vehicle by which this is meant to be achieved. The majority of the world's local authorities have initiated Agenda 21 programmes, but whilst many useful things have been *said*, very little has been *done* to implement them. This Briefing argues that the Agenda 21 project cannot succeed unless it has the full, active participation of the general public, as well as that of politicians, civic leaders and the world of business.

Sustainable development at the local level must be implemented in a holistic process which inspires city people and which gives them a sense of ownership and direct involvement. This should also include the realisation that the cities we build and the urban lifestyles we lead today will profoundly affect the chances of coming generations to shape their *own* future. Cities, as structures that are *fossilised* upon a landscape, tend to exist for a long time. But they should be *built* with long time scales in mind and the lifestyle of their inhabitants should not be defined by reckless transience. In addition to a technology and a politics of sustainability, we need to build an urban *culture* of sustainability that can be passed on from generation to generation.

What, then, is a sustainable city? Here is a provisional definition:

A 'sustainable city' is organised so as to enable all its citizens to meet their own needs and to enhance their well-being without damaging the natural world or endangering the living conditions of other people, now or in the future.

This definition concentrates the mind on fundamentals. In the first instance it emphasises *people and their long term needs*. These include good quality air and water, healthy food and good housing. It also encompasses quality education, a vibrant culture, good health care, satisfying employment or occupations and the sharing of wealth. Safety in public places, equal opportunities, freedom of expression and the needs of the young, the old and the disabled must be adequately provided for. In a sustainable city, we have to ask: *are all its citizens able to meet these needs without damaging their host planet?*

At the local level we are often more concerned with *economic* rather than *environmental* stability. In the age of globalisation, local jobs have become a rare commodity. In many towns and cities the priorities of companies, rather than democratic decision-making, determine peoples' well-being. This needs to change. Municipal authorities, as the elected representatives of local people, should play a direct role in ensuring a sense of continuity for their populace, and this should certainly include economic stability.

Environmental sustainability is very much part of this picture. It can generate jobs at the local level, by shifting the emphasis from employment in extractive industries to work in resource conservation—enhancing recycling and the energy efficiency of cities and individual buildings. Municipal authorities, on behalf of the people who elected them, should not just be concerned with street cleaning, street lights and sewage systems that work, but they should see their city as a well functioning organism that is environmentally, socially and economically sustainable. To implement such concepts, active methods of participation between municipal authorities, NGOs and neighbourhood groups need to be in place.

Today the plethora of new communication technologies should be harnessed for improving the way cities function, giving people the appropriate information to make better decisions. Urban *Intranets*, now in place in a growing number of cities, can improve communication flows between various sectors of urban society. Using the best available communication systems, we may yet learn to run our cities in more participatory ways, whilst improving their *metabolism*, and reducing their *ecological footprints*. Large cities are not going to vanish into thin air, but the way they work can certainly be much less damaging and wasteful than it is at the present time.

This Briefing is concerned with policies that could achieve these aims. It is written with three main concepts in mind, which were propounded by E. F. Schumacher: *appropriate scale, wholeness* and *connectedness*.[5] The scale at which we do something greatly determines whether we feel part of it or whether things are done 'over our heads'. Our settlements can and should be organised in such a way that we, as individual citizens, feel that we have a stake in the decisions that shape our lives. This Briefing argues that we need to look at cities as a whole—their economies, infrastructure, architecture, social networks, cultural realities and their environmental base—in order to grasp the full meaning of *sustainable urban development*.

Individually we also want to be regarded as *whole beings*, with minds, souls and feelings rather than just as people whose well-being is measured in terms of quantity of consumption. And we want to create a new sense of *connectedness*, in the neighbourhood, to people across the world, and also to future generations whose well-being is profoundly affected by decisions and investments made today.

Chapter 1

Urban Sustainability: a contradiction in terms?

City growth is changing the condition of humanity and the face of the earth. In one century, global urban populations have expanded from 15 to nearly 50 per cent of the total, and this figure is likely to increase to 60 or even 70 per cent in the next century. By 2000, half of humanity will live and work in urban areas, while the other half will increasingly depend on them for their economic survival. The size of modern cities, too, in terms of their numbers as well their physical scale, is unprecedented: in 1800 there were only two cities with a million people—London and Peking. At that time the largest 100 cities in the world had 20 million inhabitants, with each city usually extending to just a few thousand hectares. In 1990 the world's 100 largest cities accommodated 540 million people and 220 million people lived in the 20 largest cities: mega-cities of over 10 million people, some extending to hundreds of thousands of hectares. In addition, there were 35 cities of over 5 million people and hundreds of over one million.[6]

It is evident that there has been a profound change in the size of cities, their use of land and resources, and their environmental impact. Contemporary cities are very different places from their historical predecessors. They are wide open to the outside world, with road and rail systems and sea and air transport routes stretching beyond their local horizons, often for thousands of miles. A major variable is their dependence on fossil fuel (and nuclear energy) technologies to power their buildings, their factories and their transport systems.

City people have changed, too. Our evolution into 'amplified human beings'—people *amplified* by ever more numerous, more varied and more powerful technologies—occurred primarily in cities. We have changed profoundly as a result, with technologies now merged into our very being, and the experience of nature becoming ever more distant.

The physiology of traditional towns and cities was very different from that of modern *conurbations*. It was defined by production and transport systems based on muscle, water and wind power, which inevitably limited their outward and upward growth. Until the 18th century, densely populated towns ringed by defensive walls were the norm. Their historical development is also the story of the emergence of complex forms of human interaction, developing highly formalised political, economic, spiritual and military hierarchies.

The emergence of settled or sedentary urban living, with thousands of people sharing one urban space, was only possible through the concentration of food production on closely defined areas of land, a dramatic departure from hunting and gathering.[7] Urban living, to be viable in the long term, presupposes a clear understanding of conditions for sustainable human interactions with nature—an understanding that was not required before urbanisation started. Above all else, it requires the management of soil fertility and crops for the assured supply of foodstuffs to urban populations over sustained periods of time.

Early cities, such as Ur in Mesopotamia (today's Iraq) some 3,500 years ago, were themselves centres of food production. One author conjures up an image of Ur: "Most of the people we pass in the streets would be farmers, market gardeners, herdsmen and fishermen and correspondingly many of the goods transported in carts would be food products. However, some of the farmers could have had other roles as well: carpenters, smiths, potters, stone-cutters, basket-makers, leatherworkers, wool-spinners, baker and brewers are all recorded, as are merchants and what we might call the 'civil service' of the temple community—the priests and the scribes." [8]

But early towns such as Ur did not acquire their prosperity purely on the basis of urban agriculture. They also drew in resources from territories beyond, most importantly forest products. Deforestation certainly occurred on a massive scale on the hills around the cities of Mesopotamia, both for the acquisition of timber and firewood as well as for the expansion of farmland. In the case of Ur, this eventually had dramatic consequences. When Sir Leonard Wooley excavated Ur in the 1880s, he found a three-foot layer of mud that had inundated the city in around 2500 BC, and other cities in Mesopotamia suffered similar fates. The eventual decline of that civilisation is linked to a further environmental factor: the salinisation of farmland as a consequence of the injudicious use of irrigation water, with catastrophic consequences for the productivity of farm-land feeding these cities. The yields of wheat and then barley declined; eventually the only food plants that would still grow were date palms. When Europeans first travelled extensively in Mesopotamia in the 19th century they found few traces of the ancient cities: only mounds of sand and rubble in a salt-encrusted desert landscape. Are we in danger of repeating these impacts—except on a global scale?

The mode of adaptation of cities to their hinterland ultimately defines their sustainability, or the lack of it. This is strikingly illustrat-ed in the case of ancient Rome. As it grew into a city of up to a mil-lion people, its supplies of timber and food were brought in from ever more distant territories. It was Julius Caesar who decided that North Africa would be a suitable region for supplying Rome with grain, having exhausted the fertility of farmland in Italy itself, as well as that of territories elsewhere in the Mediterranean basin. Caesar's armies conquered much of the African territory north of the Sahara. It was a largely wooded landscape and one Roman writer, Pliny, mar-velled at the abundance of fruits in the forests on the slopes of the Atlas mountains and the great variety of animals. The night, Pliny wrote, was filled with the sounds of drums, cymbals, flutes—the sounds of people dancing.[9]

Roman veterans who were settled in North Africa got on with the tasks of appropriating land from nomadic tribes and converting forests into farmland. Forest timber was made into ships or houses or export-ed across the Mediterranean to Rome itself. Thousands of animals—lions, elephants, zebras, and gorillas—were captured and shipped to Rome to be put up against gladiators in the Colosseum. Some 500 towns were built in North Africa to act as epicentres of Rome's econ-omy. Their construction and their food and fuel supplies had a huge impact on the local landscape. For some 200 years, North Africa also supplied some 500,000 tonnes of grain to 300,000 Romans who were eligible for free grain, some two-thirds of Rome's total grain supply.[10]

Over the years, climate change as a result of deforestation, salin-isation as a result of irrigation, and the continued export of soil fer-tility took their toll. Around 250 AD St Cyprian, Bishop of Carthage, wrote that the "world has grown old and does not remain in its former vigour. It bears witness to its own decline. The rainfall and the sun's warmth are both diminishing; the metals are nearly exhausted; the husbandman is failing in his fields. Springs which once gushed forth liberally . . . now barely give a trickle of water." [11]

Rome's collapse occurred for a variety of reasons. Internal dissension was certainly a major factor; a lack of sustainable relationships with the environments from which it drew its resources was certainly another critical feature. At the height of its decline, between 400 and 1000 AD, Rome contracted to a town of only 30,000 people.

The German scientist Justus Liebig, a pioneer of modern chemistry in the mid-nineteenth century, was an eager student of the environmental history of Rome, and tried to understand its impact on the land supplying its food. He was particularly concerned about the way Rome had removed plant nutrients in North African soil as grain was exported from there. The minerals contained in the grain—nitrogen, potash, phosphate, magnesium and calcium—were removed from the farmland and flushed into the Mediterranean via Rome's Cloaca Maxima, never to be returned to the land. Liebig was observing the unprecedented growth of cities in the 19th century and tried to asses its impact on Europe's farmland. Would cities permanently deplete the fertility of Europe's farmland in the way Rome had done to North Africa 1800 years before? [12] In the 1840s Liebig tried to persuade the London authorities to build a sewage recycling system for the city. When they decided in the 1850s to build a sewage disposal system instead, Liebig and others set to work on the development of *artificial fertilisers*, to replenish the fertility of soil feeding cities by *artificial* means. This scientific departure contributed to the current unsustainability of both agriculture and of urban systems.

A major difference between 19th century Europe and ancient Rome was the *scale* of urban growth and its associated environmental impact. Rome, as already stated, had grown to around one million

"I have seen the greatest wonder which the world can show to the astonished spirit. I have seen it and am still astonished—and ever will there remain fixed indelibly on my memory the stone forest of houses, amid which flows the rushing stream of faces of living men with all their varied passions, and all their terrible impulses of love, of hunger, and of hatred—I mean London."—Heinrich Heine, 1827

Fertility of the Soil

The following text is from a letter by the pioneering German chemist Justus Liebig to Sir Robert Peel, Prime Minister, 1840, in the British Library Collection. It was written at a time when London's rapid growth caused great concerns about water contamination. Whilst most people were concerned about the stench of sewage in the Thames and health dangers of sewage contaminating drinking water supplies, the concerns of Liebig were primarily with the loss of plant nutrients from farmland as urban sewage was flushed into the sea:

"The cause of the exhaustion of the soil, is sought in the customs and habits of the towns people, i.e., in the construction of water closets, which do not admit of a collection and preservation of the liquid and solid excrement. They do not return in Britain to the fields, but are carried by the rivers into the sea. The equilibrium in the fertility of the soil is destroyed by this incessant removal of phosphates and can only be restored by an equivalent supply . . . If it was possible to bring back to the fields of Scotland and England all those phosphates which have been carried to the sea in the last 50 years, the crops would increase to double the quantity of former years."

people; only a few other cities in history—Constantinople (Istanbul), Edo (Tokyo) and Peking (Beijing)—reached a similar size. London's growth in the 19th century was of a new order of magnitude: in 1800 it had nearly one million people, by 1850 it reached an unprecedented population of four million. (It peaked in 1939 at 8.65 million people, with a peripheral urban region accommodating a further four million.) Cities of such vast size represented a completely new scale of urbanisation and, in addition, of human impact on the environment.

This impact is not confined to urban land use. The most pronounced difference between ancient Rome and much larger modern cities such as London is their vast use of energy. Contemporary London, with 7 million people, uses around 20 million tonnes of oil equivalent per year, or two supertankers a week, discharging some 60 million tonnes of CO_2 into the atmosphere.[13] The critical issue is whether, and how, these figures can be reduced in the process of assuring greater sustainability. Can modern cities reduce their impact on the biosphere by processes of enlightened self-regulation and self-limitation?

Chapter 2
Urbanisation and its Impacts

Many people have deplored the growth of large cities all over the world. At the 1976 Habitat Conference, the first UN city summit, for instance, a major concern was with preventing outright urbanisation from occurring world-wide. Policies were initiated to try to counter these trends and to help improve living conditions in rural areas—by supporting rural education and health programmes, improved water supplies and sanitation, village electrification and investment in rural economies. But more often than not, these sorts of policies ultimately contribute to rural-urban migration by importing urban concepts and culture into rural areas. The spread of western media to the remotest communities has further added to the process. Since the late seventies, urbanisation in the South has accelerated rather than slowed down. Only major economic crises, such as the recent slump in Asia, seem at times to dampen down further urban growth.

The global economy has grown many times over in the last 50 years and it is becoming ever more integrated. "In 1950, most of the world's workforce was employed in agriculture; by 1990 most

Ten main factors contribute to urban growth:
- national economic development
- urban accumulation of political and financial power
- import substitution
- economic globalisation
- access to global food resources
- technological development
- cheap energy supplies
- expansion of urban-centred transport systems
- migration from rural areas
- reproduction of urban populations

worked in services." [14] It is clear that urbanisation is driven above all else by economic factors, and in discussing sustainable development we have to deal with the reality of a planet that is urbanising, industrialising and globalising—at least for the time being.

Today, the world's largest and fastest growing cities are emerging in the South, because of unprecedented industrial growth there, and as a consequence of rapid changes in rural areas. Migration to cities is commonplace, particularly in places where traditional rural lifestyles are changing rapidly, and where population growth, changes in land tenure and the mechanisation of farming pushes people off the land. Development also pulls people into cities. As they grow, their impact on adjacent rural communities increases as new urban employment opportunities and the expansion of transport and communications systems attract people from outlying areas. [15]

Whilst the migration to cities can increase peoples' standards of living, it can also be a health threat for people, particularly in squatter communities, as they become exposed to high concentrations of disease vectors and pollutants. Tackling urban environmental problems, and particularly the conditions suffered by low income people, is one of the great challenges in the age of the city. [16] Many poor Third World urban neighbourhoods don't have effective infrastructures to cope with the accumulation and disposal of wastes and sewage. Rats and other vermin proliferate. Infectious diseases such as cholera, typhoid and TB, well known in cities such as London 150 years ago, are commonplace in developing cities, sometimes reaching epidemic proportions.

Urban growth is most rampant in countries undergoing rapid industrial growth. Throughout the '80s and '90s Asia, in particular, has been catching up with the per capita resource use of cities in developed countries. Until recently a few developing countries, such as China, deliberately prevented rural-urban migration by issuing local passports to stop people from moving away, but this policy is now being abandoned. Today China is probably urbanising faster than any other country in history. Like elsewhere, its urbanisation is closely linked to industrialisation. With economic growth of around 10 per cent per year, China is in the process of building some 600 new cities, [17] doubling their current number to over 1200 by 2010. Some

300 million people —a quarter of China's population, will be moving to cities, converting from peasant farming and craft-based living to urban-industrial lifestyles. But what are the likely environmental impacts of urban development in China? Increased purchasing power is already leading to greatly increased demand for consumer goods and a more meat-based diet.[18] Can soil, water and air contamination be avoided in these new cities, or will they undergo the same old 'dirty' development so familiar from Europe and North America?

The growth of modern urban economies, then, usually means two things: increased demands on the *natural capital* supplying cities, as well as increased discharges of wastes into the local and global environment. The global environmental impact of urban resource use is becoming a critical issue in the future of urbanisation and the dominant feature of the human presence on earth. As humanity urbanises, it also changes its very relationship to its host planet: global urbanisation has greatly increased humanity's use of natural resources. This can be witnessed today in developing countries, where urban people typically have much higher standards of living than rural dwellers, depending on massively increased throughput of fossil fuels, metals, meat and manufactured products. A recent study shows that a doubling of the proportion of India's and China's populations that live in cities could increase per capita energy consumption by 45 per cent—even if industrialisation and income per capita were to remain unchanged.[19] Only in countries that are 'fully' developed, such as the UK or USA, where rural lifestyles have been effectively urbanised, are levels of consumption in urban and rural areas broadly similar.

All in all, then, the growth of modern urban economies usually means two things: increased demands on natural capital and increased discharges of wastes into the local and global environment. Proposals for sustainable development have to be made in this context. The global environmental impact of urban resource use could well become the dominant feature of the human presence on earth and, given the reality of ever larger numbers of cities, one of humanity's greatest challenges for the new millennium.

Chapter 3

Cities as Superorganisms

Urban systems with millions of inhabitants are unique to the current age and they are the most complex products of shared human creativity. They are both *organisms* dependent on biological *re*-production, as well as *mechanisms* utilising mechanical production processes. Cities, and particularly large modern cities, are uniquely 'multi-layered' systems, developing extraordinary degrees of economic and social interaction. The larger a city, the more complex its system of commerce and services and the huge variety of professions associated with these.

Large cities are beehives of human activity. They have unique characteristics all of their own, with "the fine specialisation and extraordinary diversity of skills . . . firms will tend to congregate where there is a large market, but the market is large precisely where firms' production is concentrated."[20] The vast array of productive enterprise, capital and labour markets, service industries and artistic endeavour could be described as a symbiotic *cultural* system. However, as we have already seen, unlike *natural* systems, cities are highly dependent on external supplies: for their sustenance large modern cities have become dependent on global transport and communication systems. As indicated in the Introduction, this is not *civilisation* in the old-fashioned sense, but *mobilisation*, dependent on long-distance transport routes by land, sea and air.

Demand for energy defines modern cities more than any other single factor. Most rail, road and aeroplane traffic occurs between cities. All their internal activities—local transport, electricity supply, home living, services provision and manufacturing—depend on the routine use of fossil fuels. As far as I am aware, there has never been a city of more than one million people not running on fossil fuels. Without their routine use, the growth of mega-cities of ten million people and more would not have occurred. But there is a price to pay. Waste gases, such as nitrogen dioxide and sulphur dioxide, discharged by chimneys and exhaust pipes, affect the health of city people themselves and, beyond urban boundaries, forests and farmland downwind. A large proportion of the increase of carbon dioxide in the atmosphere is attributable to combustion in the world's cities. Concern about climate change, resulting mainly from fossil fuel burning, is now shared by virtually all the world's climatologists and is becoming the subject of complex new pollution trading arrangements.

The critical issue for a sustainable future is: can cities, despite their dependant status, be sustainable, self-regulating systems, both in terms of their *internal* functioning, as well as in their relationship to the *outside* world?

Urban systems are created for the exclusive benefit of humans who attempt to maintain their constant comfortable state when faced with internal or external change. It is apparent from James Lovelock's Gaia theory that biological systems are far more complex than physical ones. Unlike other feedback systems, cities, as natural, physical as well as *cultural* systems, exhibit additional layers of complexity. As centres of human social activity they are characterised by their highly developed division of labour, way beyond the fulfilment of basic human needs. Processes of deliberate and varied social interaction feature much more strongly in cities than in 'purely' *natural* systems.

Cities are industrial, trading and administrative centres, as well as markets for rural products. Given half a chance, city people develop the skills and the enterprises to organise complex economies, using ever more sophisticated production systems. "City regions, like cities themselves, pack a lot of economic life into a surprisingly small geographic compass. Copenhagen and its city regions, for example, occupy only a small portion of Denmark's territory, yet subtract them and there goes the chief part of Denmark's total economy, almost all its economic diversity, and more than half its population." [21]

Cities are predominantly centres of human co-existence, though as structures superimposed on living landscapes they also harbour a huge number of other species. But whilst cities also, ultimately, depend on maintaining a stable relationship with the biosphere, their very character as centres of intense economic activity makes them into agents for *modifying* the pre-existing assembly of life on

Forging a Global Partnership

"By the time the next century passes its first quarter, more than a billion and a half people in the world's cities will face life and health-threatening environments unless we can create a revolution in urban problem solving"—so reported the 1996 United Nations Conference Habitat II. It concluded that telling the world what it already knows can not do the job. "We need a new approach. A creative and constructive effort that only comes if we forge a global partnership between national governments and local communities, between the public and private sectors alike. We must look forward to a situation in which women, men, boys and girls can all feel personally responsible for helping shape and develop their city and for the quality of life it offers all its citizens."— Habitat II, Istanbul, 1996.

earth. Cities ultimately cannot be self-regulating superorganisms without maintaining stable linkages with the hinterland from which they draw their resources and into which they currently discharge their wastes.

Concentration of intense economic processes and high levels of consumption in cities both increase their resource demands. Apart from a monopoly on fossil fuels and metals, an urbanising humanity now uses nearly *half* the world's total photosynthetic capacity as well. Cities are the home of the 'amplified man', an unprecedented amalgam of biology and technology, transcending his biological ancestors. Beyond their boundaries, cities profoundly affect traditional rural economies and their often complex cultural adaptation to biological diversity. As better roads are built, and access to urban products is assured, rural people increasingly abandon their own indigenous cultures, which have usually been derived from a highly developed understanding of their local environment. Under the impact of cities, rural people tend to acquire urban standards of living and the mind-set to go with these.

As urban agglomerations become the dominant feature of the human presence on earth, urbanisation changes humanity's relationship to its host planet, with unprecedented impacts on forests, farmland and aquatic eco-systems. The human species is changing the very way in which the 'the web of life' on earth itself functions,[22] from a *geographically distributed* interaction of a myriad of species, into a system dominated by the resource use patterns of a *few thousand* cities. As already indicated in the Introduction, cities, built on only two per cent of the world's land surface, use over 75 per cent of the world's resources.

With Asia, Latin America and parts of Africa now joining Europe, North America and Australia in the urban experiment, it is crucial to assess whether large scale urbanisation and sustainable development can be reconciled. Whilst urbanisation is turning the living earth from a self-regulating interactive system into one dominated by humanity, we have yet to learn the skill of creating a new, sustainable equilibrium. In an urban age, can we assure that cities and their people learn to make efficient use of resources, for their own benefit as well as that of the world's environment?

Chapter 4
Cities and their
Ecological Footprint

A few years ago, on a visit to the Brazilian Amazon, I saw a huge stack of mahogany timber being loaded into a freighter at the port city of Belem, with 'London' stamped on it. I started to take an interest in the consumption patterns of cities and their impact on the biosphere. It occurred to me that logging virgin forests, or their conversion into cattle ranches and into fields of soya beans for cattle fodder (in Brazil's Mato Grosso region) or of manioc for pig feed (in rainforest regions of Thailand), was perhaps not the most rational way of assuring timber or food supply to urban 'agglomeration economies'.[23]

Contemporary cities depend on a multitude of supplies from elsewhere, and this includes land-based resources such as foodstuffs and timber, as well as of subterranean resources such as metals and fossil fuels. The way these resources are used—via processing, combustion, and disposal—has profound effects on the biosphere. A recent study by WWF shows that in the last 25 years, some 33 per cent of the natural world has been annihilated.[24] Most of resource use on the planet is for supplying cities, and most of the pollution affecting coastal waters originates from cities or from farmland feeding cities.

In order to assess the sustainability of human activity, the Canadian ecologist William Rees and his colleague Mathis Wackernagel developed the concept of the ecological footprint.[25] This they define as the land areas required to supply a city or nation with food or timber products, and to absorb its output of waste gases such as CO_2. According to Rees and Wackernagel, the ecological locations of human settlements no longer coincide with their geographical locations. However, to achieve sustainability, cities need to strive to reduce their dependence on external land areas.

Using Rees's and Wackernagel's methodology I have examined the ecological footprint of London, which also happens to be the city that started it all: the 'mother of megacities'. As the capital city

Victorian London's Demands on the Planet

"The plains of North America and Russia are our cornfields; Chicago and Odessa our granaries; Canada and the Baltic are our timber forests; Australasia contains our sheep farms; and in Argentina and on the western prairies of North America are our herds of oxen; Peru sends her silver, and the gold of South Africa and Australia flows to London; the Hindus and Chinese grow tea for us, and our coffee, sugar and spice plantations are all in the Indies. Spain and France are our vineyards and the Mediterranean are our fruit garden, and our cotton grounds, which for long have occupied the Southern United States, are now being extended everywhere in the warm regions of the Earth."—Stanley Jevons, *The Coal Question* (1865).

of an empire on which the sun never set, London took for granted the supply of resources and products from all over the world for granted. Today the empire is gone, but the city's 'ecological behaviour patterns' continue largely unchanged.

London's footprint, following Rees's definition, is vast. It extends to around 125 times its surface area of 159,000 hectares, or nearly 20 million hectares. (Britain's ecological footprint, in turn, is about eight times its actual surface area.) With 12 per cent of Britain's population, London requires the equivalent of Britain's entire productive land.[26] In reality, this land stretches all over the world.

Each Londoner, or other European citizen, currently has a footprint of some three hectares (only Americans and Canadians have larger footprints, extending to between four and five ha of land). Yet world-wide, only 1.5 ha/person of productive land is actually available. If European figures were to be applied globally, we would need two planets; if we averaged American figures, we would require three planets, rather than the one we actually have. It is clear that the ecological footprint of our cities needs to be reduced dramatically. This can be achieved—with difficulty—by improving the resource productivity of our individual consumption patterns, as well as that of the urban system as a whole. (More about that in the next chapter.)

The impact of large commercial centres such as London is, of course, not just defined by their 'direct' resource use. They are also financial services centres that have their own global impacts. Thus when discussing urban sustainability, we also have to try to assess

London's Current Ecological Footprint

Population: 7,000,000 people

Surface area: 158,000 ha

Area required for food production: 1.2 ha per person: 8,400,000 ha

Forest area required by London for wood products: 768,000 ha

Land area that would be required for carbon sequestration
= fuel production: 1.5 ha per person: 10,500,000 ha

Total London footprint: 19,700,000 ha = 125 times London's surface area

Britain's productive land: 21,000,000 ha

Britain's surface area: 24,400,000 ha

(compiled by the author, 1996)

the financial impact of urban economies on the rest of the world. A couple of years ago a friend of mine had a startling experience: "I attended a meeting typical of those which take place every day in the city of London. A group of Indonesian businessmen organised a lunch to raise £300 million to finance the clearing of a rainforest and the construction of a pulp paper plant. What struck me was how financial rationalism often overcomes common sense; that profit itself is a good thing whatever the activity, whenever the occasion. What happened to the Indonesian rainforest was dependent upon financial decisions made over lunch that day. The financial benefits would come to institutions in London, Paris or New York. Very little, if any, of the financial benefits would go to the local people. Therefore when thinking about the environmental impact of London we have to think about the decisions of fund managers which impact on the other side of the world. In essence, the rainforest may be geographically located in the Far East, but financially it might as well be located in London's Square Mile." [27]

A crucial question for world cities such as London is how they can reconcile their status as global trading centres with the new requirement for sustainable development. London's own development was closely associated with gaining access to the world's resources. How can this be reconciled with creating a sustainable relationship with the global environment and also with the aspirations of people at the local level?

This takes us to look at what sustainability means for urban businesses, which are the primary drivers in terms of urban resource consumption and economic power, from London's East India Company in the 19th century to today's transnational corporation. Businesses certainly have the desire to continue to exist. They wish to be sustainable in their own right, each in their own particular market segment and in their own particular way. The key question now is whether the momentum for sustainable development can encompass the aspirations of companies whilst achieving compatibility with the living systems of the biosphere.

Business has a vast impact on the environment. It is one of the most powerful influences on the world today, and reaches into communities around the world. Many great technological advances have come about because of business initiative, and a huge number of products and services are there for us to buy. But can business be persuaded to stop ignoring the negative consequences of its activities? There has been a great cost to communities all around the world, to the environment, and to the earth's climate.

It is certainly true that enterprises of all sizes are now becoming aware of these things. They are starting to look at their impact on the environment, and new kinds of business are starting up—ethical or green businesses. These are profitable and viable as well as having social and environmental aims. Businesses like fair trade companies guarantee a fair price to growers and producers in parts of the developing world for goods and products that we buy in the supermarket. Organic farms and food processors make sure that the food that we eat has been sustainably produced; renewable energy companies generate the electricity we use from the power of the wind, water and sun. These are the kind of businesses that are financed by social and ethical investment.[28]

There is now a green or ethical choice in most business sectors. What is really important about social and ethical investment is that it can change the way in which business is done, accommodating social and environmental concerns in the whole investment process. This can really make a difference, to business itself, as well as to the city from which it operates.

Cities are made up of large numbers of businesses. Today they have the historic opportunity to implement their own technical and organisational measures for sustainable development. They can help

Paragominas: the 'saw mill capital of the world'

The fastest growing city in the Brazilian Amazon is called Paragominas. With more than 500 saw mills, it has been called the 'saw mill capital of the world'. Between 1970 and 1991 it had an annual growth rate of 17 per cent; its population is now approaching 200,000 people, with most men working in the timber mills. Many other similar cities are emerging in the Amazon.

Paragominas sits at the centre of a road network, with tentacles that stretch deep into what used to be virgin forest. Where the tarmac ends and the mud tracks start, the economy of the city originates. Its tools are chain saws, bulldozers and vast fires—set to clear forest, on a scale equal to the recent fires in Indonesia, blanketing hundreds of thousands of acres with smoke clouds. On the road to Paragominas one witnesses the ubiquitous transformation of primary forest into a degraded landscape. Wherever urbanisation occurs in rainforest areas, cities devour forests.

Cities such as Paragominas are strikingly similar to the frontier towns of Hollywood's Wild West, places of intense local enterprise inhabited by settlers who have the gritty determination to make them into their home. But the gunslingers are never far away. Despite endemic violence, millions of people have migrated into the Amazon along the new roads built by the Brazilian government. Despite gunmen, malaria, infertile soil and hostile world opinion, the total number of settlers in the Brazilian Amazon has grown to over 10 million, with most living in cities such as Paragominas, with populations of hundreds of thousands. Some cities, such as Belem and Manaus, now have over a million inhabitants.

The economy of these cities is driven by local exchange, and national and global trade in timber, metals and beef. But as the history of the Amazon rubber boom towns earlier this century demonstrates, the very existence of cities depending on fragile rainforest resources will always be fragile.

cities to reduce their impacts on the biosphere. They ultimately have a key responsibility to help reduce the ecological footprint of cities in which they operate.

The ecological footprint concept is most useful for analysing the spatial impact of cities, and for implementing key changes in how urban systems work. One way of both reducing urban footprints and improving local environmental conditions is to introduce changes to the urban metabolism. This is the subject of the next chapter.

Chapter 5

The Metabolism of Cities

It is clear that concern about urban impacts now influences thinking at the highest international level. The need for cities to contribute to the implementation of agreements signed by the international community at UN conferences in the 1990s, is expressed in Agenda 21 and the Habitat Agenda. Agenda 21, and its prescriptions for solving global environmental problems at the local level, are well known. Building on Agenda 21, the Habitat Agenda, signed by 180 nations at the recent Habitat II conference in Istanbul, will also strongly influence the way we run our cities. It states: "Human settlements shall be planned, developed and improved in a manner that takes full account of sustainable development principles and all their components, as set out in Agenda 21 . . . We need to respect the carrying capacity of ecosystems and preservation of opportunities for future generations. Production, consumption and transport should be managed in ways that protect and conserve the stock of resources while drawing upon them. Science and technology have a crucial role in shaping sustainable human settlements and sustaining the ecosystems they depend upon." [29]

The growing understanding developed by the natural sciences of the way ecosystems function has a major contribution to make to solving the problems of urban sustainability. Cities, like other assemblies of organisms, have a definable metabolism, consisting of the flow of resources and products through the urban system for the benefit of urban populations. Given the vast scale of urbanisation, cities would be well advised to model themselves on the functioning of natural ecosystems, such as forests, to assure their long term viability. Nature's own ecosystems have an essentially *circular* metabolism in which every output which is discharged by an organism also becomes an input which renews and sustains the continuity of the whole living environment of which it is a part. The whole

The Metabolism of Greater London
(population 7,000,000)

1. INPUTS (tonnes per year)

Total tonnes of fuel, oil equivalent	20,000,000
Oxygen	40,000,000
Water	1,002,000,000
Food	2,400,000
Timber	1,200,000
Paper	2,200,000
Plastics	2,100,000
Glass	360,000
Cement	1,940,000
Bricks, blocks, sand and tarmac	36,000,000
Metals (total)	1,200,000

2. WASTES

CO_2	60,000,000
SO_2	400,000
NO_x	280,000
Wet, digested sewage sludge	7,500,000
Industrial and demolition wastes	11,400,000
Household, civic and commercial wastes	3,900,000

(compiled by the author, 1995 and 1996; sources available)

web of life hangs together in a 'chain of mutual benefit', through the flow of nutrients that pass from one organism to another.

The metabolism of most modern cities, in contrast, is essentially *linear*, with resources being 'pumped' through the urban system without much concern about their origin or about the destination of wastes, resulting in the discharge of vast amounts of waste products incompatible with natural systems. In urban management, inputs and outputs are considered as largely unconnected. Food is imported into cities, consumed, and discharged as sewage into rivers and coastal waters. Raw materials are extracted from nature, combined and processed into consumer goods that ultimately end up as rubbish which can't be beneficially reabsorbed into the natural world.

More often than not, wastes end up in some landfill site where organic materials are mixed indiscriminately with metals, plastics, glass and poisonous residues.

This linear model of urban production, consumption and disposal is unsustainable and undermines the overall ecological viability of urban systems, for it has the tendency to disrupt natural cycles. In future, cities need to function quite differently. On a predominantly urban planet, cities will need to adopt circular metabolic systems to assure their own long-term viability and that of the rural environments on whose sustained productivity they depend. To improve the urban metabolism, and to reduce the ecological footprint of cities, the application of ecological systems thinking needs to become prominent on the urban agenda. Outputs will also need to be inputs into the production system, with routine recycling of paper, metals, plastic and glass, and the conversion of organic materials, including sewage, into compost, returning plant nutrients back to the farmland that feeds the cities.

The *local* effects of the resource use of cities also needs to be better understood. Urban systems accumulate vast quantities of materials. Vienna, for instance, with 1.6 million inhabitants, every day increases its actual weight by some 25,000 tonnes.[30] Much of this is relatively inert materials, such as concrete and tarmac which are part of the built fabric of the city. Other materials, such as lead, cadmium metals, nitrates, phosphates or chlorinated hydrocarbons, build up and leach into the local environment in small, even minute quantities, with discernible environmental effects: they accumulate in water and in the soil over time, with potential consequences for the health of present and future inhabitants. The water table under large parts of London, for instance, has become unusable for drinking water because of accumulations of toxins over the last 200 years. Much of its soil is polluted by the accumulation of heavy metals during the last 50 years.

The critical question today, as humanity moves to 'full scale' urbanisation, is whether living standards in our cities can be maintained whilst curbing their local and global environmental impacts. To answer this question, it helps to draw up balance sheets quantifying the environmental impacts of urbanisation. We now need figures to compare the resource use by different cities. It is becoming

Using Waste as a Resource

What does a circular metabolism mean in practice? The town of Kalundborg, in Denmark, provides an interesting example of what can be done when waste is used as a resource rather than discarded as a nuisance. Stage by stage, local companies have developed a symbiotic system, with the waste out of one company being used as a resource by other companies. Creating a circular metabolism in which each step of the chain makes a profit.[31]

The Kalundborg process came about through entirely voluntary action by companies for commercial reasons. To a lesser extent, other cities have adopted similar resource use strategies as part of the way they operate, with the market as the main organising principle. Not all circular solutions will be market-driven, however. The creation of end-markets for waste can founder upon regulatory barriers, lack of information and scale diseconomies.

apparent that similar-sized cities supply their needs with a greatly varying throughput of resources, and local pollution levels. The critical point is that cities and their people could massively reduce their throughput of resources, maintaining a good standard of living whilst creating much needed local jobs in the process. I shall now discuss aspects of urban use of resources and energy in more detail.

A. Water and Sewage

Our cities consume vast amounts of water: in the UK, typically, some 400 litres per person per day. In the US the figure is as high as 600 litres. In older cities, such as London, water has to be pumped in from elsewhere because it is exceedingly costly to clean it to drinking water standards. Cities externalise the problem. The abstraction of river water, often many miles away from cities, has caused the destruction of river habitats and fisheries; today, many rivers supplying cities are a pale shadow of their former selves.

Water supplied to households, even if supplied from outside cities, goes through various treatment processes. River water, a major source of supply in most countries, has to be cleaned of impurities, including pesticides, phosphates and nitrates from farming. The water is percolated through sand and charcoal filter beds before

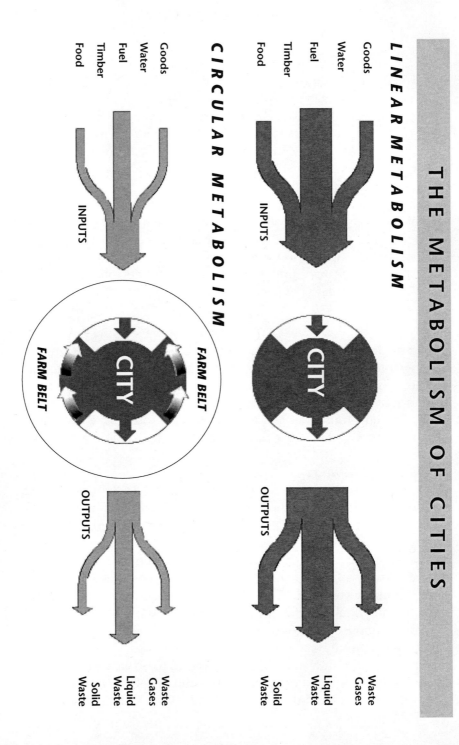

THE METABOLISM OF CITIES

LINEAR METABOLISM

Goods
Water
Fuel
Timber
Food

INPUTS

CITY

OUTPUTS

Waste
Gases

Liquid
Waste

Solid
Waste

CIRCULAR METABOLISM

Goods
Water
Fuel
Timber
Food

INPUTS

FARM BELT

CITY

FARM BELT

OUTPUTS

Waste
Gases

Liquid
Waste

Solid
Waste

it is pumped into a city's network of water pipes. Chlorination, which is commonplace, disinfects drinking water, but its unpleasant taste causes many people to switch to bottled drinking water instead. This does not make financial sense, since bottled water, at up to 60p per litre, is often more expensive than the petrol we put in the tanks of our cars. Neither does it make sense environmentally, with vast quantities of bottled water being trucked in from hundreds or even thousands of miles away at great energy cost. It would be desirable to ensure that the quality of urban water could be high enough for it to be commonly used for drinking once again.

Unfortunately, a major function of urban water supply is as a carrier for household and commercial sewage. For this and other reasons, urban sewage systems are of an important issue in the quest for urban sustainability. Their main purpose is to collect human faeces and to separate it from people, to help prevent outbreaks of diseases such as cholera or typhoid. As a result, vast quantities of sewage are flushed away into rivers and coastal waters downstream from population centres. Coastal waters the world over are enriched both with human sewage and toxic effluents, as well as the run-off of mineral fertiliser and pesticides applied to the farmland feeding cities. The fertility taken from farms in the form of crops used to feed city people is not returned to land. This open loop is not sustainable.

Whilst it is clear that cities need to have efficient sewerage systems, we need to redefine their purpose. Instead of building disposal systems we should construct recycling facilities in which sewage can be treated so that the main output is fertilisers suitable for farms, orchards and market gardens. It has been too readily forgotten that sewage contains an abundance of valuable nutrients such as nitrates, potash and phosphates. Returning these from cities to the land is an essential aspect of sustainable urban development.

A variety of new sewerage systems have been developed for this purpose using several new technologies: membrane systems that separate sewage from any contaminants; so-called 'living machines' that purify sewage by biological methods; and drying technology which converts sewage into granules that can be used as fertiliser. These technologies can be used in combination with each other, making sewerage facilities into efficient fertiliser factories. These sorts of systems are now beginning to be used in cities all over the world.

In Bristol, the water and sewage company Wessex Water now dries and granulates all of the city's sewage. The annual sewage output of 600,000 people is turned into 10,000 tonnes of fertiliser granules. Most of it is currently used to revitalise the bleak slag heaps around former mining towns such as Merthyr Tydfil in South East Wales. In contrast, Thames Water in London is currently constructing incinerators for burning the sewage sludge produced by 4 million Londoners. This is a decision of historic short-sightedness given that phosphates—only available from North Africa and Russia—are likely to be in short supply within decades. Crops for feeding cities cannot be grown without phosphates.

There is an acknowledged problem with the contamination of sewage with heavy metals and chlorinated hydrocarbons. For this reason, there is growing concern about using sewage-derived fertiliser on farmland. However the reduction of the use of lead in vehicle fuel and the de-industrialisation of our cities is reducing this problem, lessening the load of contaminants that are flushed into sewage pipes. Also, more stringent environmental legislation is further reducing contamination of sewage. The quest for greater urban sustainability will certainly lead to a significant rethink on how we design sewerage systems. The aim should be to build systems to intercept the nutrients contained in sewage whilst assuring that it can be turned into safe fertilisers for the farmland feeding cities (see also Chapter 7 on Urban Farming).

B. Solid Waste

Solid waste is the most visible output by cities. In recent decades there has been a substantial increase in solid waste produced per head, and the waste mix has become ever more complex. Today's 'garbologists' see a vast difference between early and late 20th century rubbish dumps. The former contain objects such as horse shoes, enamelled saucepans, pottery fragments and leather straps. The latter contain food wastes, plastic bags and containers, disposable nappies, mattresses, newspapers, magazines and transistor radios. But garbologists will also find plenty of discarded building materials, and crushed canisters containing various undefined, sometimes highly poisonous, liquids.

Urban wastes used to be dumped primarily in holes in the

ground. Much of London's waste, for instance, is dumped in a few huge tips, such as at Mucking on the Thames in Essex. Household waste, as well as commercial and industrial waste, is taken here by barge from central London, and 'co-disposed' in pits lined with clay. The compacted rubbish is, eventually, sealed with a top layer of clay, which is then covered with soil and seeded with grass. Inside the dump, methane gas from the rotting waste is now intercepted in plastic pipes and used to run small power stations. However, their output is quite insignificant. Mucking receives the rubbish of some 2 million people, but its methane-powered generators supply electricity to just 30,000 people.[32]

More and more cities, including London, are seeing growing resistance from people in adjoining counties on receiving urban wastes: all the environmental implications of fleets of rubbish trucks, potential groundwater contamination and stench in the vicinity of waste dumps are a growing concern. As the unwillingness to receive imported rubbish grows, other waste disposal options are urgently required. Dumping ever growing mounds of waste outside the cities where they originate is a waste of both space and resources that could be used more beneficially.

We need to think again about the ways in which urban waste management systems work. Many cities all over the world have chosen incineration as the most convenient route for 'modern' waste management. Incineration has the advantages of reducing waste materials to a small percentage of their original volume. Energy recovery can be an added bonus. But incineration is certainly not the main option for solving urban waste problems. The release of dioxins and other poisonous gases from the smokestacks of waste incinerators has given them a bad name. There have been great improvements in incineration and pollution control techniques, but only those wastes that cannot be recycled should be considered for incineration.

Recently, new objections to incinerators have been voiced in the United States because research has shown conclusively that incinerators compare badly with recycling in terms of energy conservation. Because of the high energy content of many manufactured products that end up in the rubbish bin, recycling paper, plastics, rubber and textiles is three to six more energy-efficient than incineration. These are very significant figures, given that the energy and

How Cairo Recycles its Waste

Cities in the developing world usually make highly efficient use of resources, particularly if people are supported in their recycling activities. Cairo and Manila actively encourage recycling and composting of wastes. There are a growing number of cities that are actually moving towards being zero-waste systems. Cairo, with 15 million people one of the world's largest cities, reuses and recycles most of its solid waste. Much of it is handled by a community of Coptic Christians called the Zaballeen. With the active support of the city authorities, the Zaballeen were able to acquire recycling and composting equipment. Metals and plastics are remanufactured into new products. Waste paper is reprocessed into new paper and cardboard. Rags are shredded and made into sacks and other products. Organic matter is composted and returned to the surrounding farmland as fertiliser.

The Zaballeen Environment and Development Programme has enabled the 10,000-strong community to substantially increase its income from its recycling and re-manufacturing activities. In that way, social and environmental problems affecting Cairo are tackled simultaneously. Had the waste management of the city been given over to a conventional waste management company, thousands of waste collectors would have been out of work. By helping the Zaballeen with appropriate technology, they were able to improve on their traditional waste handling methods, whilst Cairo could avoid putting vast waste dumps on the periphery of the city.[39]

In the case of solid waste management, cities in the North have much to learn from the ingenuity of waste recycling the South. Meanwhile, cities in the South could greatly benefit from the transfer of improved recycling technologies now available in the North.

resource efficiency of urban systems is regarded as critical for future urban sustainability.[33] Many European cities are now deciding against investing in new incinerators, and in favour of a combination of recycling and composting facilities instead, with minimal incineration for waste products that cannot be further recycled.

It has been said that recycling is a red herring because it is so difficult to match the supply of materials to be recycled with regular demand for recycled products. But experiences in many European cities indicate that market incentives can make recycling economically advantageous and that the right policy signals and incentives at national and local level can transform prospects. Whilst not all waste materials can be recycled, much can be done to move in this direction. As concern grows about the continuing viability of the environments on which cities depend, the reuse and recycling of solid wastes is likely to become the rule rather than the exception. Deliberately constructing 'chains of use' that mimic natural ecosystems will be an important step forward for both industrial and urban ecology.

Some modern cities have already made this a top priority. Cities across Europe are installing waste recycling and composting equipment. In German towns and cities, for instance, dozens of new composting plants are being constructed. In Sweden, Gothenburg has taken matters even further by setting up an ambitious programme for developing 'eco-cycles', minimising the leakage of toxic substances into the local environment by helping companies develop advanced non-polluting production processes.[34] Vienna also has an impressive track record, currently recycling 43 per cent of its domestic wastes.[35] This sort of figure is common to a growing number of European and American cities.

Most European cities exceed the household waste recycling performance of cities in the UK.[36] In some British cities, such as Bath and Leicester, where recycling has advanced a great deal, the benefits for people and the local environment are clearly apparent. The UK landfill tax, introduced in 1996, has increased recycling throughout the UK, helping to achieve the government target of 25 per cent household waste recycling by 2000. This taxation should be extended to approximate a recycling rate of 50 per cent, which is the target in other European countries.

In London, where currently only 7 per cent of household waste is recycled, a proposal by the London Planning Advisory Council is intended to bring recycling up to unprecedented levels. By 2000, every London home would have a recycling box with separate compartments instead of conventional dustbins. Progressively more and more municipal waste would be recycled, establishing new reprocessing industries and creating 1,500 new jobs.[37] Early in the new century, this figure would increase further. Meanwhile, the composting of organic wastes is advancing well, with 'timber stations' that compost shredded branches of pruned trees and leaf litter being established in various locations.

Throughout the developing world, too, cities have made it their business to encourage recycling and composting of wastes.[38] Cairo, Manila and Calcutta are interesting cases in point.

C. Energy

Looking down on the Earth from space at night, astronauts see an illuminated planet—vast city clusters lit up by millions of light bulbs as well as the flares of oil wells and refineries. Fossil fuels have made us what we are today—an urban-industrial species. Without the power stations they supply and the vehicles they power, our urban lifestyles and our astonishing physical mobility would not have developed.

World-wide, fossil fuel use in the last 50 years has gone up nearly five times, from 1.715 billion tonnes of oil equivalent in 1950 to well over 8 billion tonnes today. Fossil fuels provide some 85 per cent of the world's commercial energy, of which oil currently amounts to around 40 per cent. The bulk of the world's energy consumption is *within* cities, and much of the rest is used for producing and transporting goods and people *to and from* cities. This realisation is crucial for developing strategies for sustainable use of energy, particularly in the context of global warming.

Energy use is something most of us take for granted. As we switch on electric or gas appliances, we are hardly aware of the refinery, gas field, or the power station that supplies us. And despite publicity about acid rain and climate change, we rarely reflect on the impacts of our energy use on the environment because they are not experienced directly, except when we inhale exhaust fumes on a busy street.

Yet reducing urban energy consumption could make a major contribution to solving the world's air pollution problems. At the 1997 Kyoto conference on climate change, the industrialised nations agreed to cut CO_2 emissions by 5 per cent by 2010, but a world-wide cut of some 60 per cent is needed to actually *halt* global warming. As indicated in the Introduction, large cities and high levels of energy consumption are closely connected, particularly where routine use of motor cars, urban sprawl and air travel define urban lifestyles. Yet the potential exists for cities to be efficient users of energy.

London's 7 million people, for instance, use 20 million tonnes of oil equivalent per year (two supertankers a week), and discharge some 60

million tonnes of carbon dioxide. All in all, the per capita energy consumption of Londoners is amongst the highest in Europe. The city's
electricity supply system, relying on remote power stations and long-
distance transmission lines, is no more than 30 to 35 per cent efficient.
The know-how exists to bring down London's energy use by between
30 and 50 per cent without affecting living standards, and with the
potential of creating tens of thousands of jobs in the coming decades.
Significant energy conservation can be achieved by a combination of
energy efficiency and by more efficient *energy supply systems.*

In the UK, national planning regulations have already substantially improved the energy efficiency of homes, but much more can
be done. At the domestic level, two out of three low income families lack even the most basic insulation in their homes. Eight million
families cannot afford the warmth they need in the winter months.
Treating cold-related illnesses costs the National Health Service over
£1 billion per year.[40] Only one in twelve domestic properties in
Britain have the level of energy efficiency currently required by law.[41]
Yet energy efficiency's advantages are impressive—

• reduced fuel bills for everyone;
• benefits to the trade balance through curbing the need for imports;
• the creation of new jobs in the energy efficiency industry;
• the preservation of fossil fuel reserves;
• the alleviation of environmental problems, such as air pollution
and global warming, contributed to by energy generation[42]

There are many examples, particularly from Scandinavia, of how
energy efficiency combined with efficient supply systems can dramatically reduce the energy dependence of cities. There is no doubt
that the energy supply systems in many cities of the world can be
vastly improved. Take electricity: most cities are supplied by power
stations located a long way away, fired mainly by coal, with electricity being transferred along high-voltage power lines. On average,
these stations are only 34 per cent efficient. Modern gas-fired stations are slightly better, at 40-50 per cent efficiency. Combined heat
and power (CHP) stations, in contrast, are about 80 per cent efficient, because instead of wasting heat from combustion, they cap-
ture and distribute it through district heating systems.[43]

CHP systems are a very significant technology indeed. They can be fuelled by a wide variety of sources—gas, geothermal energy or even wood chips. CHP systems provide heat and chilled water, as well as electricity to urban buildings and factories. They are now common-place in many European cities. In Denmark 40 per cent of electricity is produced by CHP; in Finland 34 per cent, and in Holland 30 per cent.

Helsinki has taken the development of CHP further than most cities. Waste heat from local coal-fired power stations is used to heat 90 per cent of its buildings and homes. Its overall level of energy effi-ciency of 68 per cent was achieved because its compact land use patterns made district heating a viable option. The compactness of the city also made the development of a highly effective public transport system economically viable.[44]

In the development of CHP, the UK has been off to a slow start. Small scale systems are being installed in some office blocks, schools, hospitals and hotels, improving their energy efficiency considerably. All have the same high level of efficiency as large scale systems.

The challenge for national governments and local authorities in the developed world is to put in place new energy policies, particularly to improve urban energy efficiency. The scenario includes the creation of municipally owned and operated energy systems. In some cities, such as Vienna and Stockholm, energy systems are operated by the 'city works', which also supply water and run the transport and waste man-agement systems. The synergies possible between these services are much harder to achieve in cities where privatisation of services is the norm. It appears that the largest improvements in power distribution and consumption are realised by cities with a municipality-owned electricity company, such as Toronto and Amsterdam.[45]

The UK is just seeing the first schemes where greenhouse cultiva-tion is being combined with CHP, utilising their hot water and waste CO_2 to enhance crop growth for year-round cultivation.[46] Policies for encouraging CHP could thus also be used for enhancing urban agri-culture, bringing producers closer to their markets instead of flying and trucking in vegetables from long distances. Once again, local job creation would result (see Chapter 7 on Urban Farming).

In addition to CHP, other significant new energy technologies are becoming available for use in cities. These include heat pumps, fuel cells, solar hot water systems and photovoltaic (PV) modules. In the near future, enormous reductions in fossil fuel use can be achieved

Solar Energy in Saarbrücken, Germany

Saarbrücken, a city of 190,000 people, has a major investment programme in solar energy. Since 1986 US$1.7 million have been spent on
solar heating, PV systems, and other renewable energy sources. The state
offers a 50% subsidy for technical assistance and the local savings bank
offers residential energy users favourable lending terms for the installations. The local energy utility owns the PV array, but the inhabitants of
each house benefit from the solar electricity supply. In addition to domestic systems, there are also municipal PV installations, incorporated into
highway noise barriers. The solar initiative has the support of the entire
community because it is helping to lay the foundation for a sustainable
future. A former coal mining centre, Saarbrücken has now become a centre for the development of the urban applications of solar energy systems.

by the use of PV systems, a technology particularly suited to cities.
In the late 1990s there are only a few thousand buildings around the
world using electricity from solar panels on their roofs or facades.
Solar electricity could meet some of a building's requirements, with
the rest of the power coming from the grid.

According to calculations by the oil company BP, London could
supply most of its current summer electricity consumption from
photovoltaic modules on the roofs and walls of its buildings. While
this technology is still expensive, large scale automated production
will dramatically reduce unit costs. And the only maintenance they
require is cleaning once or twice a year.

Currently, solar energy is about 8 times more expensive than conventional, but it is expected to be competitive as early as 2010 as the
technology develops and the market grows. Major development
programmes have been announced in Japan, the USA, the
Netherlands and the European Union to stimulate market growth.
The technical potential for the generation of electricity from building integrated solar systems is very large indeed and could contribute significantly to the building energy requirements, even in a
northerly climate like that in the UK. Of course, not all buildings will
be suitable for the installation of a solar roof or façade, and adoption
will be more rapid in countries with the highest sunshine level.

Experimental solar buildings are springing up all over Europe. The new German government, elected in 1998, has a national programme for installing 100,000 PV modules. PV programmes in Japan and the USA are on a similar scale. In the UK, experimental systems have proved to be very promising. The Photovoltaics Centre at Newcastle University, a 1960s building recently clad with PV panels, has proved to be a great success. In Doxford near Newcastle, Europe's largest solar-powered office building was completed in 1998.

In the new millennium, building designers will routinely incorporate this technology when designing a new building or refurbishing an existing one. In the meantime, to get experience with the technology, governments and urban authorities should vigorously encourage the installation of PV modules in our cities, enhancing the capacity to install PV systems. Every city should have buildings to test the potential of PV and to develop the local know-how.

Another energy technology of great promise, *fuel cells*, is fast coming of age. Fuel cells convert hydrogen, natural gas or methanol into electricity by a chemical process without involving combustion. Fuel cells, like photovoltaic cells, have taken a long time to become commercially viable. Their development is now accelerating as the world searches for practical ways to produce cleaner electricity. Several companies have made great strides in making fuel cells competitive, in a variety of applications: from running generators and power stations, to buses, trucks and cars. Large scale commercial production of fuels cells will be getting under way early in the new millennium. The combination of photovoltaic cells and fuel cells is a particularly compelling option. Electric energy from PV cells could split water into oxygen and hydrogen, and the latter could be stored and then used to run fuel cell power stations, or generators for individual buildings.

It is plausible that even large cities, whose genesis depended on the routine use of fossil fuels in the first place, may be able to make significant use of renewable energy in the future. To make their energy systems more sustainable, cities will require a combination of energy-efficient systems such as CHP with heat pumps, fuel cells and photovoltaic modules, and the efficient use of energy. Regulating the energy industry to improve generating efficiency, reduce discharge of waste gases and to adopt renewables will profoundly reduce the environmental impact of urban energy systems.

Chapter 6
From Urban Sprawl to Convivial Cities

Megacities of 10 million people or more are the largest artificial structures ever to appear on the face of the earth. They are above all else the product of new transportation technologies that started to emerge in the succession in the 19th and early 20th century—steam trains, horse-drawn street cars, trams, electric underground trains, buses and suburban railways. While *travel time* for journeys remained constant, the *travel distances* increased vastly due to the availability of the new transport systems.

Urban sprawl today is above all else the result of the routine use of the motor car. From the middle of the century onwards, when low-priced motor cars further added to travel options, people were able to make individual journeys as never before. In some European countries average travel speeds have increased ten-fold in the last 40 years and distances covered have increased on a similar scale.[47] A 1991 report in a Munich newspaper graphically illustrates the astonishing volume of car traffic in this city of a million people: "Every day the nearly 700,000 cars registered in Munich, and the 500,000 daily commuters, add up to one million journeys within the city. According to an estimate by the city council, they cover a total of 14 million kilometres every single day." [48]

Urban sprawl affects most medium and large cities. It develops both radially around the perimeter of cities as well in a linear mode along major transport routes. 'Boswash', for instance, the urban corridor linking Boston, New York and Washington, is the result of such linear sprawl. Most rail and road traffic actually occurs between cities, making transport corridors the obvious locations for urban sprawl.

Motorised transport made it possible for cities to expand to hundreds of thousands of hectares, developing along railway lines and along new highways. It also assured supplies of food, forest products, manufactured goods, water, oil and gas to cities from ever greater distances. Today air transport, which starts and ends at air-ports in the vicinity of cities, further contributes to our transport and travel options.

Motor cars and public transport systems also made it feasible to zone cities into distinct residential districts, industrial zones, business centres, cultural areas and shopping malls, assuring the continued need for transport systems and increasingly replacing short distance travel on foot and by bike. By tearing apart previously spatially inte-grated functions of urban life, dependence on motorised travel was assured, building into people's daily lives travel distances that have become increasingly difficult to undo.

Given new commuting options, people contributed to urban sprawl by choosing to live in suburbs rather than in built-up city cen-tres. In the last 25 years metropolitan New York's *population*, for instance, has grown only 5 per cent, yet its *surface area* has grown by 61 per cent. Phoenix, Arizona, is the epitome of a sprawling city, extending to three times the surface area of Los Angeles despite a smaller population. LA itself is famous for sprawling along the arter-ies of its vastly complex freeway system. In Los Angeles 90 per cent of its population drive to work by car and most people live in detached houses surrounded by gardens that are often more than an acre in size. LA covers an area three times larger than London with much the same population of around 7 million. London itself, where semi-detached houses are the norm in the suburbs, is several times larger than Hong Kong, which has 6 million inhabitants and where most people live in high rise blocks. Not surprisingly, Hong Kong makes far more efficient use of transport energy and road space than London. Cities characterised by urban sprawl tend to be highly energy-inefficient.[49]

High-rise, high-density living is, of course, not everybody's idea of utopia. Some new synthesis needs to be found between compact-ness and sprawl. One thing is clear: in many cities, sprawl can be contained only by vigorously applied planning restrictions. London's outward growth, for instance, was curtailed by policies drawn up by Patrick Abercrombie after 1945.[50] A clearly defined green belt, which cannot be built on, stopped London's expansion and helped protect the rural hinterland. Similar policies are now in place in many cities in Europe, though less so in the USA. Portland, Oregon, where a successful green belt has curtailed the city's outward growth, is a notable exception.

Increasing urban density by deliberate land use policies is a key to counteracting urban sprawl. Promoting urban development that is dense enough to reduce the need for car use is seen as a vital tool for reducing urban travel. In the USA researchers found that 17 dwellings per hectare support a fairly frequent bus service; 22 dwellings support a light railway network and 37 people support an express bus service that people can reach from their homes on foot. These findings are of key importance for curtailing the use of the car.

To persuade people to give up suburbs and their quasi-rural ambience, they have to be offered urban qualities that are absent in sprawling cities: vitality, diversity, options for a wide mix of activities, social amenities and cultural facilities. In this context we have much to learn from historical cities and their lively pedestrian culture of markets, public squares and convivial meeting places. In fact, some of the most fashionable and popular urban areas, such as Chelsea, Montmartre and Greenwich Village, are all, in their different ways, places of high density and a rich mix of activities. We have to re-learn the art of building lively and safe city centres which are easily accessible on foot or by bike. We should revive the vision of cities as places of conviviality and above all else of 'settled' living. This means creating more local lifestyles within cities themselves, focusing on the concept of the urban village within the city, where community living can be a reality.

It also means reviving the street as an environment for easy human contact. In many cities, the overemphasis on providing road space just for automobiles has led to the tearing apart of community life. As traffic increases, the street loses its viability as a centre for local communication, preventing people from having regular contacts across the streets where they live.

Much thought is now being given to reviving old urban villages and to constructing new ones for the 21st century. The focus is on creating spaces with many functions, mixed neighbourhoods where people can live, work and play, where greater density creates a pattern of rich urban experience. The sustainable urban neighbourhood, as envisaged by the London consultancy URBED (Urban & Economic Development) proposes "a combination of quality space, a framework of streets and squares, a rich mix of uses, a critical mass of activity, minimal environmental harm, integration and permeability and an identifiable sense of place".[51]

In older cities there is also much potential for creating new urban villages and neighbourhoods, by a process of infill development. De-industrialisation is common to cities in Europe and North America, as companies close or are relocated to developing countries. As industries fade, cities end up with vast areas of urban dereliction. Elsewhere, land becomes vacant as ports lose their function to air-ports or container terminals, or as the older 'town gas' works are replaced by natural gas systems.

As a result, vast vacant tracts of urban space are available for redevelopment. 'Brownfield' sites offer significant opportunities for sustainable urban regeneration. Where contamination of brownfield sites is a problem, low impact methods of decontamination should be undertaken to assure minimal disturbance. The never-ending need for new homes offers the possibility for the redevelopment of inner city sites using the best available knowledge on sustainable urban living. It is crucial that redevelopment initiatives offer not only housing, but also job opportunities, community and leisure facilities, and green spaces for recreation and wildlife habitats.

Another aspect of brownfield redevelopment is that this can take the pressure off out-of-town greenfield sites. In the crowded countries of Europe, protection of the countryside has become a great concern even for city people who go there only occasionally. All the more reason to assure that protection of rural areas is tackled in conjunction with urban regeneration.

In competition with out-of-town shopping malls, inner cities have the potential to offer a much greater diversity of activities, thus becoming magnets for people of all ages. The great popularity of London's Covent Garden proves that many people enjoy pedestrian inner city spaces: to be entertained, to dine out and to do some leisurely shopping.

In addition to policies to counter sprawl, we need strategies for integrating transport systems to improve urban living. Cities such as Freiburg and Bologna have initiated major programmes of traffic reduction by exemplary integrated transport policies, greatly reducing the need for car travel. Low impact mobility within cities is greatly enhanced by trams, as the revival of such systems in Sheffield and Manchester demonstrates. Cities such as Zurich prove that a well co-ordinated tram network can get people to leave their cars at home in huge numbers.[52] But trams do not work in every context. Improved bus technology can also make a difference.

In Brazil, the city of Curitiba is often quoted as an example of well managed urban development in which forward-looking public transport planning based on buses became a central feature. In the mid-1970s, when Curitiba started to grow rapidly, the city authorities began implementing an urban design process which deliberately counteracted unplanned sprawl. It emphasised linear growth along five pre-determined structural axes.[53] The most important element shaping the city are its dedicated bus routes. Curitiba, a city of 2.2 million in 1990, has 500,000 motor cars, and yet 75 per cent of all commuters—1.3 million people a day—go by bus, because the bus system, also know as the 'surface metro', is extraordinarily well integrated. The city centre, on the other hand, offers superb pedestrian facilities and a rich mix of activities for people to enjoy. Of course many older cities, where most of the urban space is already developed, cannot easily replicate the kind of far-sighted transport planning practised in Curitiba.

It is clear that in formulating concepts for sustainable urban development we need to address the space that cities take up, reducing the distances that people have to travel and minimising the environmental impacts of travel through efficient transport technologies and the integration of transport systems. The compact city offers a model that is of great significance for sustainable urban development. Increasing density is of relevance as long as conviviality is the outcome, rather than cramped urban living conditions. It will take the ingenuity and active collaboration of planners, architects and urban citizens to insure that lively, varied, convivial and safe urban environments are created that supersede the era of urban sprawl.

Chapter 7
Prospects for Urban Farming

The same energy technologies that have made possible cities of millions of people have also led to the mechanisation of agriculture, reducing employment in rural areas whilst supplying food to distant cities via new systems of food distribution based on vast warehouses usually located near motorways, and out-of-town shopping malls. The economic boom of the last forty years has led to the assumption that city people will always *buy* food from the supermarket, not *grow* it themselves or buy it from *local* producers. This is particularly apparent as cities acquire ever greater purchasing power.

Cities have come to depend on large amounts of food being brought in from outside the land they actually occupy. London, for instance, has a surface area of some 160,000 ha, but it currently requires over 50 times its own area, or around 8.4 million ha, to feed it (see London Footprint details on page 29). Much of that land, of course, is not located in Britain itself, but in continental Europe and in countries such as the USA, Brazil, Thailand or Kenya. The largest land surfaces required for feeding cities in developed countries are for producing animal feed such as maize and soya beans to meet the demand for meat. As the world urbanises, demand for land to feed cities will continue to grow. Sooner or later, even cities such as London, which have come to take large scale food imports for granted, may need to consider reviving urban or urban-fringe agriculture to reduce the pressure on farmland.

Urban and peri-urban farming for feeding cities was the norm before bulk long distance food transport was an option. Historical cities developed effective systems for supplying food from close by. Medieval European cities, for instance, grew crops within their walls as well as on land adjoining them. They were surrounded by concentric rings of market gardens, forests, orchards, crop- and grazing land. Animals, particularly cows, were often stabled within the city and herded out to the fields in the morning and back into the city at dusk. The townspeople contributed to maintaining the fertility of the farmland that fed them by returning animal and human manure to it.

Urban farmers have always used fertile materials they found in cities for producing crops. A well known example are the vegetable growers in Paris (known as *marais*) who, until 1918, grew an abundance of crops within the city. They would heap up to 30 centimetres of horse manure on top of their vegetable beds every year, and used many ingenious methods to control soil and air temperature. They grew between three and six crops of fruit and vegetables a year, with each grower making a good living on only about three quarters of a hectare. In Paris a century ago 100,000 tons of high-value out-of-season crops were produced on 1,400 hectares, around one sixth of the surface area of the city, using about one million tonnes of horse manure. The crops were so abundant that they were even shipped to London. But the introduction of motor-powered transport ended the supply of horse manure to the *marais*, and more and more crops were brought in by train from the south of France.[54]

Today many cities in Asia continue to incorporate farming. China, in particular, has highly intensive urban cropping systems and to this day many cities are self-sufficient in food from *adjacent* land areas administered by them.[55] In Shanghai, for instance, only 20 per cent of its land is actually built on; 80 per cent, mainly in the urban perimeter, is used for crop growing, making the city self-sufficient in vegetables and producing much of the rice, pork, chicken, duck and carp. Chinese authorities are aware of the need to include urban agriculture in planning *new* cities. They are upgrading policies to enhance urban fringe farming for local consumption.

The Chinese also have a tradition of meticulously recycling and composting human and animal wastes, thus assuring the fertility of their farmland on a long-term basis. Whilst this practice has been undermined in recent years, as fertilisers have become widely available, the Chinese are now having second thoughts about abandoning it altogether. Instead they are upgrading recycling technology and are finding new, more up-to-date methods of returning sewage to the farmland.

The following examples show that in the late 20th century urban farming is a fact of life all over the world: "Singapore is fully self-reliant in meat and produces 25 per cent of its vegetable needs; Bamako, Mali, is self-sufficient in vegetables and produces half or more of the chickens it consumes; Dar-es-Salaam, one of the world's fastest growing large cities, now has 67 per cent of families engaged in farming compared with 18 per cent in 1967; 65 per cent of Moscow families are involved in food production compared with 20 per cent in 1970. For those who believe that urban food growing is commonplace only in poor countries here are examples to the contrary: there are 80,000 community gardeners on municipal land in Berlin with a waiting list of 16,000. The 1980 US census found that urban metropolitan areas produced 30 per cent of the dollar value of US agricultural production. By 1990, this figure had increased to 40 per cent." [56]

The revival of urban and peri-urban agriculture in the USA is particularly remarkable because one would not expect it in such an affluent country. Clever marketing, as well as the desire of consumers to know where their food comes from, has a lot to do with it. The rapid increase in the numbers of farmers' markets proves how popular they have become. Two thousand new farmers' markets have been set up US cities in recent years, run by growers on the urban fringes in cities such as New York, Chicago, Washington and San Francisco.

It is clear that these developments are relevant also to the UK, where too many of us still associate urban agriculture with times of desperate need. Instead, urban food growing should be considered as one of the important options for urban living.

Today there are still hundreds of thousands of allotments being cultivated across the UK. There are a variety of motives for urban cultivation: people out of work become urban growers to supply food for their families; others want to get closer to nature and to relieve stress; other people fulfil their desire for greater self-determination; and others want to contribute to making our cities more sustainable and to reduce dependence on farmland on the other side of the world.

Planners and urban administrators are often hostile to urban food growing and tend to think of it as a messy business for which there is no room in modern cities. In the UK few provisions have been made since the second world war in providing space for growing food. But at a time when work sharing is widely seen as essential for assuring a dignified existence for large numbers of people, additional opportunities for people to create livelihoods for themselves are important. Urban food growing is certainly one of the options.

Again, examples from the USA are relevant. Take New York: until a few years ago the Bronx was generally regarded as an urban disaster area, with gang warfare causing the destruction of many houses in the area. The *Green-Up Programme* is one the initiatives that has made a huge difference to the locals. Vacant lots between houses were given to community groups and turned into thriving vegetable plots by Puerto Rican and Jamaican immigrants with the application of large quantities of compost brought in from the New York Botanical Gardens.

Creating good quality soil is not usually a problem in cities: by definition they are places where fertility accumulates in great abundance, and the need to use chemical fertilisers usually does not arise. A great variety of materials is potentially available to be composted and incorporated into garden soil—kitchen wastes, old newspapers, the leaves of city trees and even human and animal faeces.

Provision of land for urban agriculture is certainly a planning policy option. In American cities such as New York and Detroit, thousands of acres of land have been given over to unemployed workers for food growing. In Britain, city farm projects have been established on areas of derelict land in some twenty cities. In Germany, land in former coal mining cities such as Essen has been set aside for urban agriculture projects.

In times of crisis, such as war or recession, growing food has always been essential to city people. Today we face a new kind of crisis: economic globalisation. Substantial unemployment is here to stay in our cities, forcing many people to adopt new survival strategies, including spending some of their time on growing food.

In cities that have experienced industrial decline, derelict land should be made available for food growing. But there has been concern about the suitability of contaminated urban land for this purpose and it is prudent not to cultivate crops less than ten metres away from busy roads. Generally, land polluted by heavy metals, such as cadmium and lead, requires special precautions on the part of growers. However, research in the USA and the UK has shown that these problems can be tackled in several ways. Firstly, maintaining a high pH by adding plenty of lime helps to immobilise heavy metals in the soil. Secondly, it is useful to add plenty of compost to the soil. People who grow food in cities tend to prefer the 'deep bed method'—creating vegetable beds in wooden or brick frames on top of the soil surface.

Not all city people will want to grow food themselves. A number of interesting approaches have been developed to create close links between growers and local customers. Urban fringe cultivation can be developed by using the model of *community supported agriculture* (CSA): in such schemes participants purchase a share in any produce in advance. Community supported agriculture is becoming popular in Europe and the USA. Participants, who pay an advance fee which entitles them to the farm's produce, also acquire the right to visit the farm and to help in the cultivation and harvesting of crops if they wish. An additional benefit is that those involved may also have a say in what crops might be grown.

Vegetable box schemes, providing customers with a selection of vegetables in season, also enjoy growing popularity. The distribution is often sub-contracted to local traders. In some cities such as Bath, Bristol and London, farmers' markets have started to appear, often specialising in organic produce. They have proved that growing crops for local consumption can be both lucrative and environmentally beneficial.

All in all, urban food growing is an important component of greater urban sustainability. Large cities will always require some food from other places; indeed they contribute to the income of people in rural areas. But the critical issue now is to establish a sustainable relationship between cities and rural areas, whilst also giving city people the option of sourcing their food from closer by, and even from within cities themselves. Food growing should be regarded as an important component of future urban living.

Chapter 8
Smart Cities and Urban Best Practice

Cities have always been centres of communication, and today electronic systems have dramatically enhanced that role. Media companies based there have a world-wide reach, using ever more sophisticated tools—satellites, digital TV, full colour newspapers and magazines. Their messages are laced with advertising, more often than not encouraging unsustainable consumption and lifestyles. Advertising itself is the main source of revenue for television and newspapers all over the world.

The global financial system is based in cities, and the financial power of urban-based institutions determines much of what happens on the face of the planet. Information technologies give urban commerce a global reach as never before. The daily money-go-round from Tokyo to London and on to New York and Los Angeles is the most striking example of this: "The new economy is organised around global networks of capital, management, and information, whose access to technological know-how is at the roots of productivity and competitiveness." [57] If this is the global network society, who controls its ever-growing power? Can the power of communication emanating from cities be exercised with a sense of responsibility appropriate to the quest for sustainability?

Making sure that cities create and maintain stable relationships with the world around them is a new task for city politicians, administrators, business people and people at large. New tools are required to help us make appropriate decisions.

One such tool is *information feedback*—putting us in a position to give account to ourselves about our impacts on the planet, and to help ameliorate these. The global power of our cities needs to be matched with an early warning system enabling us to respond as soon as unacceptable developments occur. Cities could develop *systems of 'eco-feedback'*, helping us minimise the impacts of our consumption patterns.

Eco-feedback is an evolving system of information feedback that allows individuals to influence their behaviour patterns in accordance with their own experiences. The concept was first developed by the Global Action Plan (GAP) to help householders to regularly monitor their use of energy, water and their output of waste. GAP groups help each other to modify behaviour patterns and also to reduce household running costs by making them more conscious of the environmental impact of their lifestyles and the desirability of saving money by improving efficiency.

Eco-feedback systems could also be applied publicly: for instance by displaying information on air quality, indicating when dangerous levels of air pollution are reached. Such measures could be designed to encourage people to modify their patterns of car use. This would be most effective if accompanied by incentives by local authorities to reduce the need for car travel. Eco-feedback could also be harnessed to improve the internal functioning of our cities and the communication flows between groups concerned with urban sustainability. Urban *Intranets*, now installed in a growing number of cities, could be used to enhance communication between sectors of urban society concerned with sustainability. In this context, electronic sampling of peoples' opinions for better urban decision-making should come into widespread use.

"When we build let us think that we build forever."—John Ruskin

To make the best possible use of feedback, people need a good knowledge base. For this, the most important thing is the collection and dissemination of best practices, giving people information about new options—about projects that have helped to make cities into better places. All over the world people are forming alliances to improve their local environment, to create better housing conditions and to minimise their environmental impacts.

The Habitat II Conference in Istanbul made a great deal of the fact that whilst cities are often considered as places where problems proliferate, people also want to improve their situation wherever possible. The UNCHS Best Practices and Local Leadership pro-

Urban Regeneration

In a Channel 4 TV interview, Tony Milroy described the Urban Oasis project in Salford, which transformed a run-down tower block into a revitalised environment.

"You can still see the problems faced by inner cities right here in Salford and in other high-rises all over Britain and Europe: barren wasteland, rubble, dereliction, a hostile, open environment with nothing really growing that's productive or useful. People don't own this environment. There is crime; there is no sense of security.

"Apple Tree Court was all of these things. There was a surround of concrete and jagged cobblestones; there was rubble; there was grass but very little growing. What has happened is that local people—by getting involved—have transformed themselves and have transformed this place. It's now a place of beauty and peace, with flowers, nature, a wildlife pond, vegetables and other food being grown, people feeling secure, people having a sense of ownership and privacy.

"This is quite a big area of garden and it's surrounded by a fence. There are 100 households in this block, a typical inner-city high-rise, and we divided up the garden and zoned the responsibilities. Some people are interested in the orchard area, some in growing vegetables, others in the wildlife meadow and the pond. So groups of people do what they want to do; they take an interest in it and they come up with their own ideas. This garden is the creation of the people who live here, not the result of some outside expertise being poured in with outside money.

"There are high-rises all over Britain and Europe. Either you pull them down, which is the most costly solution, or you find a way to enhance and improve them. If you can do that with the local people who live there, you can save enormous sums of money. There is not enough money around to tackle these problems, so this is a social issue and an environmental one, as much as it is an economic imperative. If you're going to solve a problem, you can't afford to do that without empowering people to do it themselves.

"What's happened here has only happened because the people who live here had a positive vision of how they could change their lives, and they've got on with it and they did it, and they learnt from it and they're proud of it."

gramme was a flagship initiative of the conference. Today it carries on with vigour, and has collected over a thousand examples from around the world which are available on the Internet;[58] and direct contacts are maintained with urban groups all over the world, reaching even some of the poorest communities. The International Council for Local Environment Initiatives (ICLEI) has also compiled a substantial body of material on urban best practices which are being disseminated through their own world-wide communication channels.[59]

Best practice initiatives cover issues such as:

• poverty reduction and job creation
• crime prevention and social justice
• access to shelter and land
• development of urban agriculture
• improved production/consumption cycles
• gender and social diversity
• infrastructure, water and energy supply
• enterprise and economic development
• innovative use of technology
• waste recycling and re-use
• environmental protection and restoration
• improved transport and communication
• participatory governance and planning
• self-help development techniques
• women's banks and local money systems

Communication using feedback is involved in all these 'best practice' examples. I believe that modern cities could develop effective cultural feedback systems, responding directly to the challenge of achieving sustainability. Active stakeholder participation is crucial to making such projects a success, and this is now widely acknowledged throughout the world's cities.

Chapter 9
Principles and Policies

The main purpose of this Briefing is to assess how to reconcile urbanisation and sustainable development. Large scale urbanisation has become an inescapable reality. We may deplore it—and many authors have done so with some vigour—but people all over the world are becoming city dwellers. Can they assure continuity for themselves and the generations which will follow them? Can their existence be compatible with the integrity of the biosphere?

Some writers have argued that large cities, particularly those with millions of people, are cancerous organisms that cannot have a permanent place on the face of the earth. We may feel that everything should be done to ensure that megacities of tens of millions of people do not become the norm, but they have become an irrefutable fact of life. Once they are there, they are homes to real people and their families, even if life may be difficult and, as is the case with many Third World cities, housing and infrastructure can be woefully inadequate.

Others argue that large cities can actually be *beneficial* for the global environment, given that vast numbers of people need to be accommodated.[60] They suggest that they make more efficient use of space than populations scattered across a landscape in small settlements. The very density of human life in large cities offers opportunities for energy efficiency in home heating, in transport and in the delivery of services. Comprehensive systems for waste management and sewage treatment are more easily organised in densely inhabited areas. And there are even opportunities for food growing: horticulture and orchards within cities and on the urban periphery, if well developed, can make a significant contribution to feeding cities and providing people with livelihoods.

This view needs to be assessed with caution. It is perhaps not surprising that the best examples of cities developing sustainable energy and waste management listed in this text are medium-sized ones, of tens to hundreds of thousands of people: cities such as Gothenburg, Helsinki, Freiburg, Portland, Saarbrüecken and Graz. 'Million cities', or mega-cities of tens of millions of people, present a much more difficult challenge for sustainable development. In future, as the conditions of their growth are reversed, they may contract again, as Rome did 1,600 years ago, though perhaps not as dramatically. Nevertheless, in the meantime they are the homes to people deserving of a 'liveable' environment, and we have to do everything we can to minimise their environmental impact.

Central and local governments all over the world are increasingly aware that comprehensive strategies for transforming cities into sustainable systems are long overdue. Whatever our views are, initiatives on sustainable development have to start with city peoples' own needs, which include:

• clean air and water, healthy food and good housing;
• quality education, a vibrant culture, good health care, satisfying employment or occupation;
• safety in public places, supportive relationships, equal opportunities and freedom of expression;
• and meeting the special requirements of the young, the old and the disabled.

All citizens should be able to meet these needs without damaging and polluting the environment, locally and globally.[61]

The task ahead is certainly huge. Governments still have little experience in the practice of sustainable urban development. Yet it is evident that they can do a great deal to initiate change by using legislation, planning regulation and public spending measures. To define contexts in which policies can be developed it is helpful define parameters for action. According to Dr. Wally N'Dow, former Director-General of UNCHS, five lessons for policy development emerged out of the preparations for the 1996 UN City Summit, Habitat II, in Istanbul.[62]

1: The power of the good examples. There are many fascinating initiatives throughout the world's cities. Habitat and its partners have helped groups from around the world to prepare reports and to make films about their own activities. It is also undertaking the dissemination of best practices. This process will deepen our understanding of urban challenges and opportunities so that realistic steps can be taken at local, national and international levels to develop new partnerships for solving problems and enriching the life of cities.

2: Complexity of issues. The contributions Habitat received also illustrated just how complex modern cities are. In this context, obstacles to successful implementation must be analysed and effective processes for implementing projects identified. In situations of rapid urban growth it is particularly important for the development of urban infrastructure problems to be overcome.

3: Local level action has large scale repercussions. For urban best practice to be transferable from one city to another, implementation must be tailored very closely to local situations. We have to ask: how applicable are best practices outside their own regions? It is particularly important to establish under what circumstances and with what types of partners successful projects have materialised.

4: Exchanges take place between peer groups in different cities. The sharing of best practice between cities is an essential tool for sustainable urban development. Once outside interest in a project has been established, site visits are of critical importance. By learning from example, local transformation can lead to global change.

5: Changing the way urban institutions work. The power of allowing people direct access to best practice examples through a dynamic process of decentralised co-operation has become very apparent. The material collected under the Habitat 'best practice initiative' is a gold mine for the world's cities and its dissemination will be of paramount importance for all the potential partners concerned.

One reality we have to deal with is that in many parts of the world, measures for sustainable urban development need to be put in place under the auspices of privatisation, which has taken the running of many urban services away from city authorities and has put them into the hands of companies. How can sustainable development occur under the auspices of privatisation? Can the self-interest of companies ever be a motivating factor? Given the right 'framing conditions', energy efficiency, well integrated transport systems and waste management can all be good for business by reducing costs. In waste management, in particular, it is clear that the outputs of some companies can be used as the raw material for other business activities. Such initiatives are certainly being developed by some cities.

In the Austrian city of Graz, the local authority developed an innovative approach to prevent pollution by introducing a closed-cycle production system similar to the recycling of materials in a natural ecosystem. The 'ecological project for integrated environmental technologies' (ECOPROFIT) highlights improved management techniques and production processes. It persuaded local companies—such as printing firms, garages, and a chain store—that it is more cost effective to avoid toxic emissions and wastes than to discharge them into the environment. Preventing pollution is advocated as superior to 'end of pipe' waste management, because the benefits include a reduction in resource consumption as well as a reduction of waste outputs. Cost saving for individual companies as well as the city authorities arise out of greater production efficiency.[63]

ECOPROFIT: Key Concepts

The producer is responsible for the whole life cycle of his product, including:

• energy consumption and emissions during the use of the products;
• its reparability, and ability to be recycled or disposed of.

Other responsibilities are as follows:

• Anything that leaves the production process should be considered as a product or raw material that can be used directly, or after processing, as an input into another production process;
• every product is optimised regarding reparability and recyclability;
• production is based on renewable sources of energy and substances that, as far a possible, are based on recycled (secondary) materials;
• the producer chooses materials from renewable resources and releases wastes in a way that does not diminish nature;
• the producer minimises the energy demand to a level that can be provided by renewable energy sources.

ECOPROFIT is a partnership between the municipality, the technical university and the private sector. The reduced pollution benefits business as well as the municipal authority which is charged with the delivery of services, including drinking water, waste management and environmental remediation. Information and technical assistance to local companies is coupled with marketing support. To facilitate a preventive approach, information offered to companies has proved more effective than regulation. Incentives to minimise pollution are important to get firms to participate in the scheme. They include the promotion of participating companies to the local community as 'ecological market leaders'.

In the delivery of services, too, market-led decisions themselves can sometimes contribute to efficiency improvements. In the UK, for instance, the privatised power industry has made substantial investments in efficient gas-fired power stations that have stabilised Britain's output of waste gases. But much higher efficiencies are possible. Real incentives are now needed for the power industry to invest in efficient inner city CHP systems and solar energy technologies.

The formulation and implementation of policies for urban sustainability under the auspices of privatisation is certainly new territory for politicians, administrators, business people and people at large. Many players are involved—national and local government, companies and private individuals—which complicates matters. But the time is ripe for real breakthroughs in this area. More often than not, the parameters of what happens locally are determined by national planning policies, and approaches to these are very different in city-owned systems as compared to market-led systems such as in the UK.

Overall, parameters set by government regulation and legislation are clearly important for improving resource productivity and reducing the environmental impacts of cities and companies operating within them. The UK's landfill tax is a case in point: it has led to increased investment in recycling by privately owned waste management companies, making the achievement of the government target of 25 per cent household recycling by 2000 more plausible. But further incentives are certainly necessary to transform a disposal-based waste management system into one based on waste minimisation and full circularity.

Eco-friendly urban development could well become the greatest challenge of the twenty-first century, not only for human self-interest, but also for the sake of a sustainable relationship between cities and the planet. Limiting urban resource consumption and waste output will certainly be critically important for an urbanising humanity to be viable in the long term. The many varied aspects of sustainable urban development need to be integrated into a set of interlocking policies that can be applied under widely varying circumstances.

We have many options for sustainable urban development: waste prevention, reuse and recycling can facilitate an efficiency revolution in *resource consumption*. Efficient and clean energy systems can improve the performance of cities and their buildings. Eco-friendly architectural design can further reduce urban environmental impact. Investment in resource extraction, conservation and recycling will create new employment and business opportunities where they are most needed: in environmental technology industries.

Transport technologies, too, are due for a major overhaul. Super-efficient low emission vehicles are already becoming available. In some cities, even where people had come to depend almost exclusively on private transport, rapid urban transit systems are starting to reappear. But it is above all else changes in urban land use that

Involving Young People

"Why is it so important to involve young people in appreciating these ideas of sustainable development? Young people will inherit the urban future that is currently in the making. In many countries they constitute a very large proportion of urban populations. In 1992, world youth population was one-third of total world population. Out of this, 84 per cent lived in cities. Many young people meet the sunset of their opportunities at the dawn of their existence, with unemployment and insecurity leading to crime, violence and drug abuse. Yet they are entitled to a healthy and productive life of social peace and equal opportunities in harmony with the natural world. It is therefore crucial for young people actively to participate in decision-making on the issues that affect their lives today and in the future. This also means having a say in investments in education, training and job creation that can effect their future positively. Their energy, intellectual capacity, and ability to muster support for urban initiatives is crucial for generating meaningful change." Habitat II, Istanbul, 1996.

are needed: enabling city people to reduce the need for travel in the first place.

These aims can ultimately be achieved only by vigorous public participation and pressure. To assure that such policies are developed and adopted, popular participation is of the greatest significance. The democratic process is indispensable for generating changes on the scale that are needed.

To help cities to develop and implement viable sustainability policies, key questions have to be asked. Questions such as: Does my city—

• compile an annual environmental report?
• use life cycle analysis in its own purchasing decisions?
• support public environmental education?
• create jobs from environmental regeneration?
• practise comprehensive waste reduction and recycling?
• have policies for transport integration and pedestrianisation?
• have plans to develop a sustainable energy system?
• encourage ecological business?
• support ecological architecture and new urban villages?
• encourage urban agriculture and farmers' markets?
• create wildlife sanctuaries?
• avoid the use of timber from virgin forests?

The time may have come to develop a 1 to 10 rating system for the performance of local authorities on sustainability issues. This would benefit citizens, help local authorities to learn from each other's experiences, and deepen the understanding on the most useful national policy frameworks for enhancing urban sustainability.

Expertise in ecological urban regeneration is now widely available. The critical issue is to develop the capacity to apply it in the real world and to do so involving the general public, business, NGOs and local authorities in active partnerships.

The greatest success stories show that enlightened civic leadership, together with a general public determined to make real changes, and an active partnership with local business, can move mountains.

It is clear that individuals are motivated in such initiatives primarily by the wish to improve their local environment and to generate tangible improvements in their own lives, and not just by the desire to create a better future for the planet. It is also clear that suitable national and international policy frameworks are of crucial importance for improved local sustainability.

Cities with a high degree of local self-determination and with the capacity to raise local taxes for sustainable development are usually better placed to make real changes. Typically, countries with vigorous democracies, often involving proportional representation, have got furthest with improving their cities.

All in all, creating sustainable cities is one of the great challenges for an urbanising humanity at the threshold of the new millennium. Since most human activity now revolves around cities and their economies, it is critical to get things right. This text is an attempt to contribute to the process.

Chattanooga Vision 2000

Chattanooga, Tennessee, was a 'first generation' industrial city, with coal mines, coke plants, foundries, and a federal ammunition plant. In the 1960s things started falling apart. Deindustrialisation caused growing unemployment, bad housing contributed to racial tension, a legacy of pollution led to bad public health.

In 1984 the city authorities, business and civic leaders started 'Chatanooga Venture—A Decade of Vision' to facilitate the community's involvement in developing a new agenda for the city. 'Vision 2000' persuaded 1700 people to define new goals, hopes and practical dreams and to formulate 40 goals. They then went on to create projects, task forces and organisations to implement specific actions. 790 million dollars were raised to invest in the community through a variety of public/private partnerships. By 1992 37 of the 40 goals had been implemented through 223 separate programmes and projects. All this created a new 'can-do atmosphere' in the city.

In the same year ReVision 2000 was launched to build on the Vision 2000 initiative. 2600 people participated. A further 27 goals were formulated. Further improvements to the city's physical environment were initiated. A clean-up of industrial pollution using the national 'Superfund' programme got underway.

Today Chattanooga is recognised as a leading 'Environment City'. Good housing for all is being largely achieved. New environmental industries, including factories for electric buses and a carpet recycling, have created many new jobs. Highly effective waste water treatment, including interception of toxic liquids by factories, has been established. An exemplary waste recycling system has been established in the city. Its natural beauty has been enhanced in a great variety of ways.

Chattanooga has gone further than most cities in a process of environment-led regeneration. It has initiated a vigorous participatory process involving thousands of people. Significant linkages are being made between environmental, social and economic sustainability.

Chapter 10

A Culture of Sustainability

There is little doubt that many of the world's major environmental problems—and indeed social problems—will only be solved through new ways of managing our cities and leading our urban lives, and through vigorous public participation in decision-making and implementation. Cities are nothing if not centres of knowledge, and today this also means knowledge of the world and our impact upon it. Reducing urban impacts is as much about education, information dissemination and participation as about the better uses of technology.

This is ultimately a cultural issue, concerned with the way in which knowledge is disseminated and passed on from generation to generation. Cultural development is a critical aspect of sustainable urban development, giving cities the chance to realise their full potential as centres of creativity, education and communication. Ultimately that cannot be done without changing the cultural values underpinning our cities.

As I have suggested, cities need to endeavour again to become centres of *civilisation*, not of *mobilisation*. We need to implement the vision of cities as a places of creativity, of conviviality and above all else of settled living. Cities can be places of beauty, with great public spaces and buildings, as well as places for intimate community living.

The greatest energy of cities should circulate *within*, generating masterpieces of human creativity—not be drawn from *outside*, bringing in ever more products from ever more distant places. The future of cities crucially depends on the utilisation of the rich knowledge of their people, and that includes environmental knowledge. Cities cannot claim to be knowledge-led without activating the know-how to beautify their own internal environment for all to enjoy and to reduce their impact on environments world-wide. They are what their people are. If we decide to create sustainable cities,

we need to create a cultural context for this. In the end only a profound change of attitudes, a spiritual and ethical change, can bring
the deeper transformations required.

Thought has created the unstable world in which we now live—
manifested in mega-technology, mega-cities, global power structures and vast environmental impacts. Practical visions and working
examples of innovative, alternative systems are now urgently needed. We need new, practical thinking on sustainability, peace and personal empowerment. By emphasising *human-scale* solutions we can
contribute to a core transformation of contemporary urban culture.
We now need to develop concepts for *real sustainability* to bring
about the reconciliation between cities, their people and nature.
These efforts need to:

• involve the whole person—mind, spirit and body
• place long term stewardship above short term satisfaction
• ensure justice and fairness informed by civic responsibility
• identify the appropriate scale of viable human activities
• encourage diversity within the unity of a given community
• develop precautionary principles, anticipating the effects of our
actions
• ensure that our use of resources does not diminish the living
environment.

It is clear that we need a revolution in urban problem solving—
for the sake of cities themselves as well as to reduce their impacts on
the world. We need new approaches to urban planning and management and vigorous new partnerships between national governments, local authorities, urban communities, NGOs and the private
sector.

Whether it is the environment or human rights, poverty, population growth or the status of women, we must deal with these issues
in our cities. That is why they have become a priority challenge for
the international community; why it is essential that they are at the
centre of a growing global effort to make our communities productive, safe, healthy, more equitable and sustainable.

It is crucial to extend popular participation in decision-making to
restore confidence in local democracy. Consultation is not enough.
To strengthen local democratic processes, methods such as neigh-

The Sustainable City

The sustainable city is:

• *A Just City*, where justice, food shelter, education, health and hope are fairly distributed

• *A Beautiful City*, where art, architecture, and landscape spark the imagination and move the spirit;

• *A Creative City*, where open-mindedness and experimentation mobilise the full potential of its human resources and allows the fast response to change;

• *An Ecological City*, which minimises its ecological impact, where landscape and built form are balanced and where buildings and infrastructures are safe and resource efficient;

• *A City of Easy Contact and Mobility*, where information is exchanged both face-to-face and electronically;

• *A Compact and Polycentric City*, which protects the countryside, focuses and integrates communities within neighbourhoods and maximises proximity;

• *A Diverse City*, where a broad range of overlapping activities create animation, inspiration and foster a vital public life.

From Richard Rogers, *Cities for a Small Planet*, Faber and Faber (1998).

bourhood forums, action planning and consensus-building should be widely used, because in appropriate circumstances these lead to better decisions and easier implementation. With the help of modern communications technologies, wider citizens' involvement can be incorporated into strategic decision-making.

Eco- and people-friendly urban development could well become the greatest challenge of the twenty-first century, not only for human self-interest, but also to create a sustainable relationship between cities and the biosphere. Ultimately that cannot be done without changing the value systems underpinning our cities and, more broadly, our national cultures. In the end, it is only a profound change of attitudes, a spiritual and ethical change, together with new political attitudes and economic practice, that can assure that cities become truly sustainable.

If we get things right, cities in the new millennium will be centres for a culture of sustainability. They will be energy- and resource-efficient, people-friendly, and culturally rich, with active democracies assuring the best uses of human energies. Prudent infrastructure development will enhance employment, improving public health and living conditions. In northern mega-cities, such as London and New York, enhanced sustainability will contribute significantly to employment. In cities in the South, significant investment in infrastructure will make a vast difference to health and living conditions.

But none of this will happen unless we create a new balance between the material and the spiritual, and to that effect much good work needs to be done. A calmer, serener vision of cities is needed to help them fulfil their true potential as places not just of the body but of the spirit. The greatest energy of cities should be directed towards creating masterpieces of human creativity.

Organisations

All these organisations are involved in urban sustainability initiatives. Further information can be found on the World Wide Web.

International Council for Local Environment Initiatives (ICLEI)
Local Agenda 21 Initiative, City Hall, East Tower, 8th Floor
Toronto, Ontario, Canada M5H 2N2
www.iclei.org

ICLEI European Secretariat
Eschholzstrasse 86, D-79115 Freiburg, Germany

ICLEI is the probably most important international organisation working on sustainability issues. It gives advice to cities on practical measures to improve their local environment as well as reducing their wider environmental impact. It organises international conferences.

UK Local Agenda 21
Local Government Management Board
Arndale House, Arndale Centre, Luton LU1 2TS, UK

The UK Local Agenda 21 process was selected as an 'international best practice' in the run-up to the UN Habitat Conference in Istanbul, 1996. It gives support to LA 21 initiatives across the UK.

The European Sustainable Towns and Cities Campaign
Rue de Treves 49-51, B-1040 Brussels, Belgium

This Campaign publishes a most useful newsletter and organises conferences on sustainable urban development. It has contributed significantly to putting the issues discussed in this briefing on the European Union agenda.

UNED-UK
3 Whitehall Court, London SW1A 2EL, UK

UNED-UK has an impressive track record in influencing the wording of international agreements such as the Habitat Agenda. It has done much to develop indicators for sustainable urban development.

Healthy Cities Project
World Health Organisation
8 Scherfigsvej, 2100 Copenhagen, Denmark

The Healthy Cities Programme of WHO is a pioneer in developing the urban health agenda. It is increasingly linked to urban sustainability initiatives around the world.

United Nations Centre for Human Settlements (UNCHS)
PO Box 30030, Nairobi, Kenya
www.bestpractices.org

This is the primary UN organisation working on urban sustainability issues. Its Sustainable Cities Programme works with cities throughout the world. Its Best Practices programme has compiled a global dossier on environmental and social sustainability initiatives.

United Nations Development Programme
1 United Nations Plaza, New York NY 10017, USA

UNDP has developed its own initiatives on urban sustainability, particularly by focusing on technical expertise in low impact transport, infrastructure and industrial development.

Appendix II
References

1   David Satterthwaite in UN Centre for Human Settlements, *An Urbanizing World*, Oxford University Press, Oxford, 1996.
2   as 1.
3   Herbert Girardet, *The Gaia Atlas of Cities*, Gaia Books, London, 1992 and 1996.
4   Steven Gorelick, *Small is Beautiful, Big is Subsidised*, International Society for Ecology & Culture, Week, Dartington, 1998.
5   E.F. Schumacher, *Small is Beautiful*, Abacus, London, 1973.
6   as 1.
7   Richard B. Lee and Irven Devore, *Man the Hunter*, Aldine, Chicago, 1968.
8   Ruth Whitehouse, *The First Cities*, Phaidon, Oxford, 1977.
9   Quoted in Susan Raven, *Rome in Africa*, Longman, London, 1984.
10 as 8.
11 V.D. Carter and T. Dale, *Topsoil and Civilisation*, University of Oklahoma Press, Norman, 1974.
12 Justus Liebig, *Agriculturchemie*, 9. Auflage, Vieweg Verlag, Braunshweig, 1876.
13 see figures on page 33.
14 Wally N'Dow in Uener Kirdar, ed., *Cities Fit for People*, United Nations Publications, New York, 1997.
15 as 1.
16 Jorge Hardoy, Diana Mitlin & David Satterthwaite, *Environmental Problems in Third World Cities*, Earthscan Publications, London 1992.
17 Worldwatch Institute, *The State of the World*, 1996, Earthscan, London, 1997.
18 ibid.
19 Joseph Romm and Charles Curtis, 'Mideast oil forever?', *The Atlantic Monthly*, April 1996.
20 LSE Greater London Group, *London's Size and Diversity*, January 1996.
21 ibid.
22 Fritjof Capra, *The Web of Life*, Harper Collins, London, 1996.
23 as 18.
24 *The Living Planet Index*, WWF, 1998.
25 Mathis Wackernagel and William Rees, *Our Ecological Footprint*, New Society, 1996.
26 Herbert Girardet, *Getting London in Shape for 2000*, London First, 1996.
27 Mark Campanale, personal communication.
28 Susan Jenkins, Triodos Bank, from an interview with Channel 4 TV, London.

29   The Habitat Agenda, UN, New York, 1996.
30   Prof. Paul Brunner, TU, Vienna, personal communication.
31   *Business Week*, Green Business Guide, 1997.
32   Western Riverside Authority, Annual Report, 1991-92.
33   *Worldwatch Paper 121*, Washington, 1994.
34   ICLEI, *The Local Agenda 21 Planning Guide*, Toronto, 1996.
35   Dr. Gerhard Gilnreiner, Vienna, personal communication.
36   Prof. Gerhard Vogel, Vienna, personal communication.
37   *Evening Standard*, London, 30 December 1996.
38   *Warmer Bulletin*, London, Summer 1995.
39   *The Mega-Cities Project, Environmental Justice, Promising Solutions at The Intersection of Environment and Poverty*, New York, 1994.
40   National Energy Action, Newcastle, 1997.
41   Energy Savings Trust, *Meeting The Challenge To Safeguard Our Future*, London, 1992.
42   Energy Savings Trust, London, 1992.
43   Combined Heat and Power Association, London, 1998.
44   as 34.
45   Peter Nijkamp and Adriaan Perrels, *Sustainable Cities in Europe*, Earthscan, London, 1994.
46   *Grower Magazine*, 21 March 1996.
47   Hermann Knopflacher, *Zur Harmonie von Stadt und Verkehr*, Boehlau Verlag, Wien, 1993.
48   *Sueddeutsche Zeitung*, Munich, 21 April 1991.
49   Newman and Kenworthy, *Cities and Automobile Dependence*, Avebury 1989.
50   Peter Hall, *London 2000*, Faber and Faber, 1963.
51   URBED, *The Sustainable Urban Neighbourhood*, fold-out brochure, London, 1997.
52   as 3.
53   Jonas Rabinovitch in Edesio Fernandes, ed., *Environmental Strategies for Sustainable Development in Urban Areas*, Ashgate, Aldershot, 1998.
54   Kropotkin, *Field, Factories and Workshops*, Transaction Publishers, USA.
55   Victor Sit, ed., *Chinese Cities: the growth of the metropolis since 1949*, Oxford University Press, 1988.
56   UNDP, *Urban Agriculture*, New York, 1996.
57   Manuel Castells, *The Network Society*, Blackwells, Oxford, 1996.
58   www.bestpractices.org
59   www.iclei.org
60   Richard Gilbert in Richard Gilbert, Don Stevenson and Herbert Girardet, *Making Cities Work: the role of local authorities in the urban environment*, Earthscan, London, 1996.
61   From: John Jopling and Herbert Girardet, *Creating a Sustainable London*, 1996.
62   Quoted in Herbert Girardet, *The Gaia Atlas of Cities* (see 3 above).
63   as 34.

SCHUMACHER BRIEFINGS

The Schumacher Society is now extending its outreach with the Schumacher Briefings—carefully researched, clearly written and well designed 20,000 word booklets on key aspects of sustainable development, to be published three times a year. They offer readers:

• background information and an overview of the issue concerned
• an understanding of the state of play in the UK and elsewhere
• best practice examples of relevance for the issue under discussion
• an overview of policy implications and implementation.

Current Briefings are as follows:

The Briefings are published by Green Books on behalf of the Schumacher Society. To order a subscription, or for further details, please contact the Schumacher Society office (see right)

THE SCHUMACHER SOCIETY
See the whole, make the connections, identify appropriate scale

The Society builds on the legacy of economist and philosopher E. F. Schumacher, author of seminal books such as *Small is Beautiful, Good Work* and *A Guide for the Perplexed*. Guided by his intensely practical as well as spiritually informed vision, Schumacher wanted to give societies, communities and individuals appropriate tools for change. The Schumacher Society promotes human-scale solutions for an enhanced relationship between people and the environment.

At the heart of the Society's work are the Schumacher Lectures, held in Bristol every year since 1978. At the lectures, distinguished speakers from all over the world discuss key aspects of the sustainable well-being of people living in harmony with the earth. Speakers have included Amory Lovins, Herman Daly, Petra Kelly, Jonathon Porritt, James Lovelock, Wangari Maathai, Matthew Fox, Sir James Goldsmith, Susan George, Patrick Holden, George Monbiot, Maneka Gandhi, James Robertson and Vandana Shiva.

The Society is based in Bristol. It is a non-profit making company limited by guarantee. We can receive charitable donations through the Environmental Research Association based in Hartland, Devon.

Schumacher Society Members receive:

- Discounted tickets at the Bristol Schumacher Lectures
- Two Schumacher Briefings as they are published
- Two Schumacher UK Newsletters
- 10% discount off cost of courses at Gaia Coach Institute
- 5% off cost of courses at the Centre for Alternative Technology
- The catalogue of the Schumacher Book Service

And your subscription will be supporting our work.

The Schumacher Society, The CREATE Centre, Smeaton Road, Bristol BS1 6XN. Phone/fax: 0117 903 1081.
www.schumacher.org.uk